And So We Move On!

And So We Move On!

NIGEL TREVELYAN

StoryTerrace

Text Nigel Trevelyan

Edited by Georgia Rajah, on behalf of StoryTerrace

Design StoryTerrace and Jelena Žarko

Copyright © Nigel Trevelyan and StoryTerrace

Text is private and confidential

First print March 2021

StoryTerrace

www.StoryTerrace.com

To Flora, without whom this book would never have been written. Your advice and enthusiasm invaluable, your support absolute. You are just amazing.

CONTENTS

PROLOGUE

All I could hear was the rain, incessant, a continual cascade of water pouring off a narrow makeshift roof onto the sodden dirt, winding its way in rivulets into the road. My watch said 5am and I was cold, sheltering under a corrugated iron lean-to that provided my five-star accommodation for the night. I began checking Cynthia (my bike, of which more later). Having cycled to the outskirts of Hanoi, I had by my reckoning some forty kilometres to go. My mind wandered. Vietnam was the 116th country I had visited, quite an achievement I thought. The previous day had been challenging to say the least. After a long day's ride, I had left the bike unlocked overnight in a partly covered porchway with me alongside and managed an hour or two of disturbed sleep whilst keeping watch.

have spent a great deal of my life travelling, from an early age it has been something that has always driven me. I was never interested in the traditional five-star treatment. I wanted to experience what life was like for people across the world and understand what shaped a nation. I have been incredibly fortunate to have enjoyed good health throughout most of my life. By luck or design, I have also managed to engineer long career breaks. I became a specialist in my profession and chose a job that did not involve a close team environment, which meant I had a fair chance of re-employment upon return. Each time I left, I never knew if I would ever come back. I was open to the idea of ending up in some far-flung place as a surveyor or doing who-knows-what. Many people live their lives vicariously through TV and books, frequently because circumstances dictate that that is the way things must be. Few have the good fortune or opportunity of choice to do what I did. I chose to live my own life, free from the shackles of social convention. Like many, I never really knew what I wanted to do as a career, I was appreciative that money did not grow on trees and had to be worked for, but I was never ambitious, except in wanting to travel to as many countries as I could. In that regard, it made several important decisions much easier.

1

THE EARLY DAYS

The Doctor's face was stern. "I'm sorry" began his words, conveyed to my mother, "I don't expect your baby to survive the night", I was then only four weeks old. But survive I did, and I have often thought that that prognosis, frequently relayed to me by my mother, gave me the will and desire to grab life with both hands and live each day as if it were my last. It was down to the tenacity of one doctor who, in a last ditch attempt to discover why I could not take food or nourishment, said he would have just one more look at the x-ray. It turned out that there was a blockage in my oesophagus that prevented me from ingesting food naturally.

Left with a constant reminder, by way of an abdomen scarred by a series of stitches (that resembled an O Level knitting class), my silent mantra from then on was 'I can do it'. Another unlikely source of inspiration was my home background, which was a claustrophobic mix of a father with whom I had nothing in common and a mother who was too busy trying to be everything to everyone. I often felt that my father was unhappy, he had his own battles to fight, and so my mother took it upon herself to keep us apart whilst also attempting to retain the peace between me and a domineering mother-in-law. Ah Grandma, she who held the purse strings in terms of apportioning favouritism and treats between my sister and I; she who insisted that each mouthful of food should be chewed forty times; she who lived with us for far too long! They said to respect your elders, I never ever adhered to that philosophy. Respect, I learned from an early age, had to be earned. Back then, my bike was a means of escaping as quickly as I could from the stultifying environment at home.

The move to Bridgwater in the 1950s was due to a transfer for my father, who was employed with Barclays Bank. In those days such transfers were routine and commonplace, invariably from one end of the country to another, unlike today. It was a career that never suited him. As a young man he had wanted to study Chemistry at University but his parents, as was often the case in those days, chose a safe and secure career path for him that guaranteed a pension. They refused to send him to University, to his detriment.

It was evident from early on in my life that I had little common ground with my dad. As such, communication was stilted and increasingly limited to a "hello" or "goodbye" with not much in between. He never asked how I got on playing football in a school match and I never asked about his work or what music he played on the piano.

The situation was exacerbated in the early 1960s when Grandma (Dad's mother) came to live with us, she stayed until she died in 1967. A simply dreadful woman, I despised her! She was a nasty piece of work and a complete hypocrite who went to church twice a week and thought that would buy her a first-class ticket upstairs. Meanwhile, she displayed little Christian charity on a day-to-day basis and certainly not towards me. It was obvious that she preferred my sister, she would regularly give her sweets and treats in front of me. In fairness to my sister, she never made anything of it.

In those days, the main meal was at lunchtime. We often had to sit at the table until my grandma had finished. Lunch would frequently last more than an hour and a half (one course)! I had to watch my friends playing around the house, waiting for me to receive permission from my parents to leave the table. My grandma's extensive chewing habits were deliberate I'm sure. She relished the fact that I would have to sit and endure interminable mealtimes, instead of joining my friends to go trainspotting on our bikes or go fishing or play football.

Underneath, it had all become too much. In the half hour it took to walk home from Wembdon Primary, I used to dream and imagine what my life would be like once I left home. I was very unhappy, and this began to manifest itself physically. It all started when I was eight, while I was waiting in line at Miss Sadler's desk to get my sums marked, I suddenly felt very dizzy and fainted. Within a few weeks I was in Musgrove Park Hospital in Taunton, wired up for sound and given a lumber puncture for good measure. The registrar who carried out the procedure did not enjoy a favoured bedside manner and I formed the impression that he quite enjoyed inflicting a bit of pain here and there. The diagnosis was severe migraine, and I was told that eventually I would grow out of it. What the registrar did not say, was that without any warning my surroundings would start to rotate around me. I had to lie down with the curtains drawn and be subjected to a heavy snow shower in front of my eyes for up to two days. It was quite common to get two episodes a month, more sometimes. These constant dizzy spells lasted with me until I was well past sixteen and of course they had quite a profound effect on my childhood. Playing sport was restricted, I could not stand for any length of time, I couldn't head a ball and I hated being surrounded by a lot of people. The medical diagnosis, I subsequently learned, was likely to have been a reaction to the situation at home.

Gradually, as I got older and wiser, I learned to adapt and develop a skillset to overcome the stress of homelife. I began to pre-empt mealtimes, ensuring I was out of the house by 8am. I would get on my bike, cycle to Bridgwater Station and spend the days trainspotting with my friends who would join me at around 9am. There was no breakfast TV in those days. I would often look at each train and imagine all its different destinations, I would spy people in the carriages and wonder where their journey was taking them; the possibilities were endless. Railways have continued to provide a lifelong interest along with supporting Plymouth Argyle F.C. I have no sense of pain!

Depending on the time of year, my friends and I would all meet up to go fishing for the day; a particular favourite was Screech Owl ponds on the outskirts of Bridgwater. Here we could fish and train spot at the same time, since the main Bristol to Plymouth line ran close by. These were the best times, away from the house. I frequently used to imagine what I would end up doing with my life and somehow travel was never far away.

2

AND SO WE MOVE ON

Finding Cynthia

Most people might assume that at sixty-one, life might take on a more temperate pace. I might become more settled, with maybe a bit of golf or bird watching before retirement. Even at sixty-one, I had no desire for the armchair or an easier life. I wanted another challenge. I pulled out the world map one evening and studied it. What if? Could I? I began researching and considering possible routes across various countries. Sitting with a glass of scotch over Christmas 2011, I thought, 'well I haven't cycled much'. And so, the seeds were sown.

At the time, I didn't even own a bike, so what made me think this was a good idea? I liked the idea of a challenge, but it did seem a bit extreme. As the ideas began to ferment, I started making a few notes and researching the type of bike I would need. I was overweight, but that was not an issue as I knew that once I got going it would soon come off. Questions, questions! What would be my route? How long would I need? Like many ideas, you can over plan and the whole thing gets more complicated as you end up tying yourself in knots. Having become something of an expert in the art of rough travel over the years, I wasn't fazed by overplanning. I decided to first sort the right bike, then choose the first place to cycle to, after that I would let nature take its course. My mantra: don't make any grand gestures about doing this or that, just do it, whatever 'it' amounts to. Whilst I was not fit, I had no intention of undergoing a physical development programme. For me, this was just a bike ride, it might end up a bit longer than the average, but a bike ride was all it would be.

There have been multiple facets to my life. As a young boy I would spend my time standing on platforms watching locomotives thundering through; as a young man I spent time in the Merchant Navy; and in later years my travel ventures took off at great speed. Looking back, I think these experiences, along with this cycle venture, all held the common denominators of adventure and exploration. Not that I was afraid of a more staid and conventional way of life, although I never wanted that, but from a very early age I always felt there was so much more out there. The world was a place to explore, to seek out different countries and cultures. To the best of my knowledge, I was only on this planet once and I planned to make the most of it.

I have always been a restless spirit, fortunate to have travelled considerably throughout my life. Over the years my thirst for travel and adventure has never been quenched and it's never been far from the surface either. Travel and adventure are like drugs to me. I have always had this desire to experience life from outside this protected shell in which we now exist and observe the diversity of landforms, places and ecology which this wonderful planet offers. The thrill of travel is to wake up in the morning, not knowing how the day's events will unfold or where you will end up in the evening.

Why did I decide to attempt to cycle as far as I could go? I was no lycra cyclist. I occasionally rode my Trek 7.3 hybrid, usually in lightweight trousers and a tee shirt, rarely more than a few kilometres at a time and with no religious fervour regarding target distances or time limits. The bike had spent most of its time in the garage. I knew enough about cycling to recognise that a trip of such magnitude would require a far sturdier beast. So, the research began and as with any cycle or vehicle there were many in a particular class to choose from. I tentatively looked at the Dutch Kuga, which according to many long-distance cyclists enjoyed a good reputation for reliability. The more I researched the easier the decision became. Fortunately, the British still made the best of many things and a long-distance touring bicycle was one of them. Thorn was based in Bridgwater, Somerset, and it had built up an international reputation on a whole range of touring bicycles.

I decided that I needed Thorn's expert advice to pick the right bike and spec. Thorn was to bicycles what Savile Row was to suits. I telephoned initially, explaining my intentions, and was invited to their premises to test various models for suitability and to fine tune my requirements regarding the composition of the bike. Arriving in St Johns Street in Bridgwater was a novel experience. I had grown up in the town and knew it well, a couple of shops along was the angling shop (formerly Ray Perretts) where half my childhood was spent along with the railway station further down the road. Behind Thorn's shop front was a huge complex where the bikes were built and tested. I had a 30 minute chat, during which time we narrowed the choice of bicycle down to two. I took out both bikes and rode them around the street to get a feel as to how they handled. Given the weight I was likely to be carrying and the terrain, I settled on a Nomad Mark 2. I chose the bright yellow steel frame 26" Rohloff equipped bike, with 14 gears set to a ratio that suited me and the terrain I was likely to encounter. Initially it was fitted with 1.75" tyres although I carried a set of Marathon XR 2.25" tyres which were bombproof for the rough stuff. I chose a Brooks leather saddle, which I was assured would soften with wear and time. In the end, the saddle didn't work for me. The studs came through after a few weeks and riding became uncomfortable to say the least! The pedals were clip ins, I never felt happy with them either and as with the saddle, they became another casualty on my journey. The Nomad could carry 30kg at the rear which together with the front bags enabled a load of some 50kg in total. I started with 42kg and finished up with about 23kg, which said a lot about what I needed or didn't need in different parts of the world and also how I adapted to cycling conditions and life on the road over time. After collecting Cynthia (named after my ex-mother-in-law) from Thorn, I brought her home and in preparation for the journey ahead I rode her between 40 – 70km a day, approximately three times a week, which was nothing excessive. If I had any issues, I called Thorn and they gave me as much time and help as I needed.

Made of steel and requiring careful handling while exuding an underlying fondness, were characteristics I associated with my bike. They were also qualities attributable to my ex-mother-in-law. I first met Cynthia over the bar at the Lee Bay Hotel, near Ilfracombe. Her family had not long moved into the area and on a summer's evening she would wander down to enjoy a few tequila sunrises in the bar overlooking Lee Bay. Displaying a somewhat dominant personality, she did expect people to fall in with well-established arrangements. Christmas was always a case in point where diplomacy was high on the agenda. She feigned offence when I likened her bread sauce to the texture of the M5 but invariably took it in good spirit. Like her namesake, my bike, when handled carefully, responded well and my affection for her increased as the journey unfolded. Cynthia was a good name for the bike, it suited her well.

A common theory when packing panniers or a suitcase, is to lay out everything you think you will need, then divide it by two, then halve again. Even then, the chances are you will still have too much. Briefly, I packed the following:

- Single tent
- Sleeping bag
- Small Swedish stove with pan
- First aid and dental repair kits plus sundry creams etc
- Leatherman penknife, compass, Katadyn water bottle and filter
- Cycle spares: 2 x Marathon XR 2.25" tyres, puncture and repair kit, six spokes
- Clothes: 1 pair of lycra shorts, 2 x tee shirts, 1 pair of socks, 2 pairs of underpants, 1 x hoodie (Children with Cancer logo), 1 pair of light trainers, 1 x thin waterproof top, 1 pair of clip-in shoes
- Maps of Europe and Asia

I had no defined route or plan, which was probably unusual, certainly among cyclists. Speaking to those on the road, many had plans that were set in stone with a firm timeframe in place. I was fortunate to have travelled so much over the years, as it meant that I had a fair idea of what to expect. I also had no time limit; it was more a question of when the money would run out, although I had calculated I could last quite a while so that was not an immediate issue. I wasn't certain if cycling was going to suit a 60+ body! So, I decided to set myself small goals to start with, although in the back of my mind, I had a broad route in mind that took in countries which I had not visited before. I decided that my first goal upon reaching the Continent would be Amsterdam.

3

THE EARLY DAYS

Leaving Home

At the age of eleven I wrote to Canada House, asking for information about Canada and what I would have to do to emigrate. One morning, after having waited for what felt like an interminable amount of time for a reply, the postman knocked and presented me with an enormous package with 'Canada House' emblazoned across it. Dashing upstairs, I closed my bedroom door and opened the parcel. Inside were numerous pamphlets and booklets describing opportunities and life in Canada, including a wonderfully illustrated book referencing each of the provinces. This became mandatory bedtime reading and the book was never more than an arm's length away in my bedroom. At that tender age, I decided that as soon as I could I would emigrate to Canada and become a Park Ranger. I used to wish my life away waiting for that moment.

It is hard enough realising you are an adolescent and all that that brings, and then suddenly testosterone begins coursing through your veins like a river in heavy flood. I was not an attractive lad, quite the opposite, I was overweight (my mother decided the one way she could make me happy was to feed me all the wrong stuff, which I enjoyed), I wore glasses, was very shy and somewhat preoccupied with the day-to-day challenge of keeping my migraines under control. Inevitably as young teenagers do, they let slip that they fancy someone. I had a crush on a girl who wore brown school uniform. I'd see her every morning at the bus stop, on the opposite side of the road by the Odeon, waiting to catch a bus to St Margaret's. If only Vanessa Pidgeon knew the effect she had on me… of course, inevitably she did! The boys waiting at my bus stop constantly took the mick and baited me, "Go on Nige, get over there, chat her up". I was too shy to accept the challenge, not that I would have known what to say or do if I had. An older boy, John Bird, who thought he was the coolest guy on the planet, with a Vespa Scooter adorned with more mirrors than you could shake a stick at, decided to take matters in hand. He accelerated across the road and screamed to a halt in front of the group of girls waiting at the opposite bus stop. I just prayed their bus would come at that exact minute, but it didn't. The reply naturally enough was a blank and my last view of the scene outside the Odeon that morning, as I sat on my own bus, was of several girls giggling around the object of my desire.

Having passed the 13 Plus, I left Westover Secondary Modern and went to Brymore School, an agricultural Day/Boarding school in Cannington, near Bridgwater. The move suited me reasonably well, as although I didn't enjoy school, it at least got me away from homelife as I was able to stay on as a dayboy after 4pm every day. I'd finish prep and join in with the evening sports activities with my mates before cycling home, then on a Saturday I usually played rugby or cricket for the school. I held limited academic aspirations, partly because of the severe migraines which made it almost impossible to focus continually on schoolwork, but also because I struggled to keep up in what was a less than academic environment at home. I just needed to be outdoors as much as possible. My satchel invariably contained railway and travel literature which I used to slip into textbooks to relieve the boredom from Trollope, Leviticus, trigonometry, French translation or whatever happened to be on the timetable for the day.

At home I indulged in all the wrong food, encouraged by my mum who thought she was doing me a favour in her role as peacemaker. Consequently, my weight steadily increased. No one had yet made the connection that rich foods and migraines didn't go well together! I am sure my mum thought she was doing the right thing, after all I didn't have to eat everything. By the time I was sixteen my weight had ballooned to sixteen stone and I could not be described as a racing snake on the rugby field. In fact, I was struggling badly to keep up. Fortunately, I was popular at school and got on ok with everyone. Two of my best mates got hold of me on one cold day in January on the rugby field and told me I needed to lose weight.

It was during my final year at Brymore when I heard that Dad had been offered a transfer to Ilfracombe in Devon, much to my sister's dismay. She was doing her O Levels at Bridgwater grammar school and was a highflier, the brains of the family. The transfer meant she had to leave to attend Ilfracombe Comprehensive, whose academic standing was something much less to be desired. I learnt in later life that she was absolutely fuming with our parents at the time for taking this decision, which was virtually a sideways move for our father in any case. We couldn't understand why they would have jeopardised their daughter's education at such a critical point in life. Despite her efforts, she did not achieve the grades she would have at Bridgwater and her choice of A levels had to change. Fortunately, she got over that hurdle, and later achieved a First-Class Honours at Liverpool University and completed a Doctorate in Egyptology. The move to Devon meant that I became a border which suited me fine.

At boarding school, I focussed on shedding my excess poundage and enlisted the help of the two friends who had drawn me aside. Having taken the decision quite publicly to lose weight, I single-mindedly set about the challenge. From 16 stone plus in January, I fell to 12 stone 3 lbs by the beginning of May. I knew this because it was written on my school report. Such was the dramatic impact, I found I could run and run well. As the trials for the summer house athletics day approached, I decided to enter for the 440 yards. In the heats (there were two heats for this race), I went up against a lad who was a year older and was the clear favourite to win. It was my first competitive race so, tactically, and having never run a 440, I had no idea. I just decided to go for it and stay with the leader for as long as I could. There were five in our heat and coming around the final bend I was slightly ahead of the favourite and a good twenty yards clear of the rest, he had enough in the tank though to pip me on the line. Although I was not a fan of coming second (who remembers who came second!), the race was pivotal in my thinking at the time. OK I got beaten, but I was not expected to come anywhere other than last. It showed me what might be possible if I made the effort to change myself, whether that meant adapting physically or mentally to improve my situation.

At last, the summer of 1968 came around, the final term of school arrived and with it the thought of exams but also freedom afterwards. I was still feeling the effects of the migraines and the last thing I wanted to do was study, I found concentrating so difficult. I had also developed something of a rebellious streak which came to the fore at this time. This manifested itself in February when I applied to P&O to join the Merchant Navy. During the spring term we had the usual visit from the careers officer where each of us had an interview and filled out a few forms. Most of the lads were heading back to help run the family farm. The conclusion they drew from my information and interview was that I should be a salesman. When I told my parents, they thought it was a good fit! I remember just wondering if they ever really knew anything about me. Travel had always been a motivation, which the career officer clearly chose to ignore. Perhaps they thought selling widgets somewhere in the South West would satisfy my wanderlust! There was a great big world out there and I wanted a lump of it.

I attended an interview some weeks later at the offices of the Peninsula and Oriental Steam Navigation Company in Aldgate, London. As I entered the portals there was a huge picture of the then Chairman, Jeffrey Stirling, and a wall covered with photographs of the passenger fleet. The interview went well, and they called me back a month later for a second interview. Options were discussed. If I achieved 5 O Levels, I could think about joining and training as a junior officer. Fine, but knowing 5 O Levels was beyond me (I had effectively given up on education) and also knowing I would be accepted as a rating, that was good enough and it suited my purposes well. In the intervening period I read and studied all the brochures, so I knew the liners and the routes. In May I was offered a position as a waiter on the Oriana, one of the top two liners in the fleet alongside her larger sister the Canberra. I would be joining in January

1969, around my eighteenth birthday and the first trip was a six and a half month round the world voyage including two 'boomerang' cruises from Australia. The acceptance of that appointment killed any lingering enthusiasm I had for educational attainment and so it proved when the results were posted through the door.

My final few weeks at Brymore were not covered in glory. The usual high jinks accompanying the end of term had begun and unfortunately, I was caught trying to raid the adjoining dorm by way of a sheet hanging from our own dorm window. Our dorm overlooked the Headmaster's house, and we were spotted. Hauled before him the following morning after assembly, I was marched into his study, trousers down, given six whacks and invited to leave school early. It was time for me to join the outside world.

Between August and January my auntie, who was a wonderful lady, held a high powered job as PA to the Managing Director of British Transport Hotels based in Paddington. The Group owned several of the prestigious railway hotels attached to the main London stations and hotels on the major golf courses including St Andrews, Turnberry and Gleneagles. After she pulled a few strings, I caught the Flying Scotsman at 10am one Friday from Kings Cross and eventually arrived at The Old Course Hotel in St Andrews at 6.45pm to be told to change as I was due to work in the restaurant at 7pm. My departure from the hotel in January did not go down too well as they thought I was there for the whole three years under a training programme. I didn't realise until some while later, that my auntie had got me that position assuming I would decide not to go to sea. I did feel bad about that when I found out.

On the appointed day in January 1969, having turned eighteen, with a ticket in hand, I caught the train from Woolacombe. As it passed Redbridge on the outskirts of Southampton, the railway ran parallel with the docks and along the number of piers where the ocean liners berthed. I looked across and saw the funnel and superstructure of the ship, with the name 'Oriana' set above the shed in front of her. I had no fear at all, just excitement and anticipation for what might lie ahead. Members of my family had all told Mum and Dad that I was making a big mistake and would end up "queer" or a "drug addict". They thought I should get some qualifications and a job with a pension. I did not care what anyone said, I knew me, and this was the start of my life.

4

AND SO WE MOVE ON

How About a Cycle Ride?

Shortly after turning 61, I decided to let my cottage near Budleigh Salterton in March 2012. I moved briefly to my sister's place in Cheltenham and it was there that all the pieces of the jigsaw came together. In May, after a brief three week preparation period, my right foot engaged the toe clip, my right leg pushed down, and the first revolution of my journey was complete. I cycled some fifty yards to the main road and turned left, and, as I did so, I took in one last sight of my sister and mother who were waving, not knowing whether it would be days, weeks or months before I saw them again, or maybe never. The plan was to set off from Cheltenham to Harwich, where I would take the overnight ferry to the Hook of Holland and start from there with Amsterdam as the first destination. Even at this point, while I had a rough idea as to where I was heading, I still had no specific route in mind. Flexibility and choice were the name of the game, although I had set myself a series of small targets ultimately with the goal of cycling around the world. The preparation period enabled me to put in a few kilometres on Cynthia, my bike, and I was able to get used to her many idiosyncrasies.

I had contacted local press throughout the West Country, letting them know that I was planning to cycle the world unaided and that I hoped to raise a few bob for the Children with Cancer Charity. In truth, I was somewhat reluctant to go all out on a full marketing campaign as, not being a serious cyclist, I had no idea how far I was going to get, and I knew there would be no chance of sponsorship. In the end, the charity very kindly provided me with tee shirts and other items to publicise the effort. When I cycled away from Cheltenham, I had no idea what I was letting myself in for. Questions sped through my mind; how long would this last? Would I make it to Harwich? Would I fall off going up the hill before I had even left Cheltenham and look a real idiot?

Settling into the carriage seat, having loaded Cynthia somewhat unceremoniously in the bike rack, I watched as we pulled away from the remainder of Cheltenham Spa station and gathered speed. My thoughts regressed to when I was just 18, when I looked up from the train and saw the ochre funnel and superstructure of the P&O liner SS Oriana. The sense of anticipation, adventure and apprehension as the train passed her by was overwhelming. I had no idea what was ahead and like the journey I had just begun, that was the thrill.

The decision to use public transportation to Harwich was taken so that I did not waste a few days cycling through bad weather in England. It didn't matter where I started, so I thought the Hook of Holland was as good as any. After arriving in Paddington I hauled Cynthia off the rack, having waited for the majority of passengers to get off first, and made my way towards the station exit. I settled in the saddle and set off across London to Liverpool Street Station. It was not the easiest ride, especially as I was unfamiliar with the local geography and London traffic. I thought it would be good to test the balance of the bike and weight distribution from how I'd packed the panniers. I was quite pleased as she rode well, although it took a few corners to get to grips with the way Cynthia responded. Liverpool Street Station was not an easy place to find or access, and when I did it was 6pm and the middle of rush hour, the place was a heaving mass of humanity. I manoeuvred my way in, walking carefully, I tried to avoid bumping into people, but it was more a case of people bumping into me in their lemming-like dash to break away from the city. I tied Cynthia up to a pillar within eyesight and joined the queue for a ticket. I decided quickly that there was no point trying to negotiate my way further through to the platform, it would be much better to catch a later train even if it meant hanging around for an hour or two. I eventually caught one that departed at around

7.30pm. Getting Cynthia on and racked up was no mean feat, the carriages were still crowded with standing room only. With assistance from a guard, we awkwardly hoisted, and half dragged the bike into the right carriage, I stood close by for the whole journey.

The weather was good, it was a warm late spring evening, and I watched the fields pass by, wondering how long it would be before I set foot back in England. I looked at the people around me, tired, heads in books and wanting no eye contact with anyone. The evening papers were discarded as people left the train at their appointed stop. Very few spoke to each other. I remember thinking how fortunate I was, to be starting this new adventure, whilst all the commuters would be back doing it again tomorrow. The train pulled into Harwich International just after 9pm. It was relatively easy to get off as most people had left the train en route. I made my way to the Stena Line terminal building in good time and booked a cabin. Fortunately, the ferry wasn't full so I had a cabin to myself. After passport control, I was directed onto the ferry. I fastened Cynthia up on the car deck along with several other touring bicycles and made my way up on deck. After thanking the barman, I carried my beer to a window seat overlooking the town. This was it. I was off at last and it felt like the start. I remained in the bar as the engines began with a gentle shuddering as the ship's moorings were released. The gap between land and ship grew wider as her bow turned to face the English

Channel. I just kept looking forward, towards Holland.

My wristwatch alarm sounded. I could hear the bow thrusters gently nudging the vessel parallel with the berth. After a quick shower I was up on deck to look at the dock area on the New Waterway, opposite and to the south west of which was the city of Rotterdam. Making my way down to the car deck, I saw Cynthia fastened to the bulkhead. With my overnight things back in the pannier, I checked everything over and unfastened the lock and ropes that had held her secure. The ramp lowered and we were waved off, several of the cyclists had no gear whatsoever and took off at a rate of knots.

Following the exit signs, I guided Cynthia out of the port area before stopping to look at a signpost showing several bike routes. On the advice of a couple of cyclists I met on board, I followed the coastal road north. While heading to The Hague, I skirted around the fringe of the city and cycled onwards through the university town of Leiden. As I drew further inland towards Amsterdam, I looked at the mileage on my bike computer. I had only completed 64km in a day and felt shattered. The adjustment to cycling, the weight and balance of the bike came as a shock to my body. That night, I camped in a field and ate bread and cheese plus some chocolate I had bought on the way. My initial feeling was 'what am I doing?' which was tempered by the fact that I knew I would shed body weight and get fitter as the journey progressed. I just had to take each day as it came. My meal was also an indication of how I was likely to consume food. At the end of the day, did I really want to get cooking and clear up after? It was possible I would think differently in time.

Packed and back on Cynthia, I passed a sign saying 'Amsterdam 5km'. It was a small achievement, but it felt great! I had attained my first goal to Amsterdam, and Holland had proved to be the best place for me to start. The topography was flat, so it was ideal to build my legs up and get them used to cycling. The country had a dedicated network of bike routes, which allowed me to cycle away from the traffic, and each route had clear markings at regular intervals showing distance figures. Despite my appalling sense of direction, it was easy to find my way around with a map.

Soon into my journey I found that establishing a new regime was the hardest problem to deal with, as well as the need to build a decent rhythm into the day and the ride. I learnt quickly to prioritise putting in the hard yards, at the expense of every sightseeing opportunity. Amsterdam was a beautiful city, however, I only stayed a day as it was their public holiday and there was no hostel accommodation to be found anywhere. Heading north I passed through Edam, an attractive, typical Dutch town, with tree lined avenues alongside canals. The Dutch countryside reminded me of East Anglia. There wasn't a scrap of rubbish anywhere and beautiful gardens were carefully manicured, most inevitably had canal frontage. Just south of Groningen, I decided to turn and head south east into Germany. I had originally intended to head north to Denmark and Sweden, but my plans changed due to weather and time constraints. A large low pressure was tracking from the south west, so I set my target for Prague.

In Holland and throughout much of Germany I wild camped, occasionally stopping on a site. While a hot shower was tempting, I had nothing dry to put on. The weather, which I had been following closely, hit hard with torrential rain that started as I cycled over the German border, it continued non-stop for several days. The waterproof gear I carried was of little use in such relentless and torrential conditions. I was hit from above and underneath through puddles and spray and was wet from rain and sweat that had merged together. Once the tent was up, I dried my gear as best as I could and climbed into a wet Alpkit sleeping bag (a superb piece of kit). In the morning, I would listen for the patter of rain on the tent and say to myself "remind me why I am doing this?". Then I would pack the tent, which was usually sodden, with the rest of the kit, put my wet cycling gear back on, and head out on the road once again. It was so cold that I had to wear four layers and buy an extra fleece. After arriving in a small town, a local resident in the bakery took pity on me and kindly opened up what I took to be a village hall. She let me stay there for the afternoon and night, it felt like luxury accommodation after what I'd been through. I didn't need much persuading to accept the accommodation, as there were towels, hot water and hot radiators. The storm was into its seventh day and the chance to dry my clothes and camping gear was not to be missed. I was able to pick up a good takeaway and so, additionally armed with loads of cakes and buns, I made myself comfortable for the night. The following morning, I handed back the keys and thanked my host as I was packing up the panniers. The storm gradually blew over and the rain eased.

The next day I continued with my journey and crossed into Germany, although no one would ever have known I had, since there was no sign to say 'Welcome to Germany'. I cycled towards Haren and then followed a route along the central south east corridor, which passed through the Lower Saxony town of Hamlyn. The town was beautiful and very affluent historically. It was better known for the Grimm Brothers tale of the local Authority reneging on its promises! Afterward, I spent an afternoon in the thriving and attractive university city of Göttingen. Like Holland, Germany delivered on some excellent cycle routes, some of which followed the rivers, like the Weser, around Hamlyn. Although the routes increased my mileage, the scenery made the detours all the more worthwhile.

During one of my stays at a campsite I met up with a German men's netball team. As I was putting up my tent, they came over, introduced themselves and invited me to join them at the campsite bar to watch the Germany v Portugal game. Politics is not something a traveller really wants to get involved with in a guest country, but they were keen to know how we, the Brits, perceived Germany, which I found a surprising question. I reassured them that our respect for their work ethic and quality of product was high on the list. Surprisingly, for their generation, they were unconvinced about Europe and despite their country's economic dominance I could sense a certain underlying insecurity, which seemed strange. I formed the impression that they were not huge fans of France either, which made me feel that if their views were held similarly on a national scale the portents for the future of the European Union perhaps faced some challenges.

After two weeks passed, and I had dried out from the rain, the whole idea of cycling took on a much more positive dimension. Added to which, my fitness was improving, and I was adding more mileage by the day. Halfway through Germany, I crossed into the former East Germany. Even with the war long gone, it still retained a perceptible difference in affluence and architecture. Villages and small towns were generally set amongst the undulating countryside and they still had edifices of the former Soviet style buildings that were no longer used. There were numerous similarities in the architectural style to Kazakhstan, where I had previously worked. Perhaps they had borrowed the same Soviet architect who had built many of the buildings in the pre-unification era.

Towards the Czech border the topography became hilly and the scenery improved, I found it similar in many ways to Exmoor. Bavaria lay close to the border and consequently the buildings began to reflect that, being constructed of traditional wood. Nestling in the vicinity was a city called Plauen. Plauen, like Hamlyn, had developed its affluence from the lace industry. Seventy five per cent of the city had been flattened during the war and was subsequently ignored pre-unification. I found it to be a delightful city, rebuilt with inordinate character. The trams made their way through the main streets and the people were particularly pleasant. Its claim to fame alongside Leipzig, was that between them they started the movement for unification. There was little love for their former eastern bloc regime.

I took the train for the 50km journey between Plauen and Cheb in the Czech Republic, preferring to cut through the hills rather than go over them. It took a further four days from Cheb to Prague, which was only 174km. In a similar vein to Holland and Germany, cyclists in the Czech Republic were encouraged to take B roads or cycle paths, however I found that the terrain was extremely hilly, and the paths were indistinct. In many cases I'd find myself travelling through a mix of dirt and forestry tracks, which were wholly unsuitable for a poor road bike like Cynthia. 1 in 6 elevations up these tracks was not unusual so hauling the best part of 48kg was not a lot of fun. I found my expected journey time doubling with ease, Cynthia and I trudged on and I took it to be part of life's rich pattern and the challenge I had set us. However, within the hills between Cheb and Prague I found a little spa town called Karlovy Vary which was beautiful and provided just the lift I was looking for.

I wild camped all the way through the Czech Republic. There were plenty of opportunities to erect the tent and disguise the bike away from the roads. I had decided some time previously that after a day's cycling I did not want to cook, so I made do with whatever I could eat along the way. On one occasion I arrived at a small service station which had a café. Unfortunately, the café was closed, but the proprietor very kindly made me coffee and provided an assortment of rolls and cakes. It looked like rain was starting to settle in (not for the first time) so I asked if it would be possible to pitch my tent onsite. He was fine with that and just asked that I left before 8am. I began pitching my tent behind the main building, which had the only piece of grass, and the smell of oil and petroleum pervaded. On closer inspection, it was evident that the area had been used for dumping fuel of one sort or another. The rain started, so I quickly found a sheltered spot on the café concrete forecourt that remained unobserved from the road. I lay my sleeping bag down and covered myself with the tent as you would a blanket. It wasn't an ideal situation, and by 5am, whilst it had stopped raining, it was darn cold! The temperature was certainly a sufficient incentive to pack fast and get the circulation moving as quickly as possible.

After I left the service station, I made good time and found myself on the outskirts of Prague on a Sunday morning at around 8am. I still had about 30km to go. My map of Europe did not exactly have the detail I was looking for to navigate my way into the centre, but that was nothing new. I passed a residential estate, at the junction of which I met a cyclist. It transpired he was an Englishman who was living and working in Prague and he was a very keen cyclist. He was just setting off, but very kindly adapted his route to show me the way into the City. It turned out that he followed the Tour de France and a few of his mates had cycled one of the mountain stages in last year's Tour. Aged about thirty, he showed no sense of frustration at my speed compared to his. He asked if I had an address for a hostel, which I had, and rode with me up to about 2km from the hostel. On one of the bridges spanning the Vltava River we went our separate ways.

I looked towards the city with some sense of satisfaction. I had achieved the second goal. My fitness levels were good, I had certainly shed a lot of weight and I was now confident that I could cover the mileage to anywhere. On half decent roads I was cycling between 80km and 120km a day (90km was a fair average). My lowest day's mileage was just before Karlova Vary, where I managed only 40km. It was mostly on foot and over awful hilly forestry terrain. Did I want to stop? There was no question in my mind that I wanted to continue. Whilst looking out from the bridge, I made the decision to rest and stay two nights in Prague before heading to İstanbul. At least then I could say I had cycled across Europe.

I found Prague to be a beautiful city. At its core was the Old Town Square, which was surrounded by colourful baroque buildings and narrow streets leading off in all directions. It was easy to walk around, and I found that the city was well worth the stop over. It helped that the beer was within budget too! One of the signs that you are in the zone on a bike, is that peddling does not become all consuming. I frequently found myself enjoying the scenery, taking everything in. Peculiarly, songs started springing to my mind, frequently, songs that I would least expect, but seemed to match the rhythm of my day. I cycled a memorable few kilometres with a local gentleman of 73. He was very fit and told me, in excellent English, that he raced for the Czech Republic and even competed in the milk race in 1962. Apparently, he made it up Porlock Hill (a 1:4 climb) near Minehead (my current hometown) without stopping!

By now I had surmised that Cynthia was a major piece of work! Fully laden, she still wandered all over the place and needed firm handling from the saddle. My bike had lived up to her namesake and only weeks into the ride she continued to draw similarities with my ex-mother-in-law! Overall, she (the bike) behaved impeccably. The pedal crank came off in Cheb, but it was an easy job to screw it back in. Then, probably as a result of the bike falling down some steps in Karlovy Vary and a subsequent rough haul over mountain bike tracks, the rear wheel split at the side. I was able to fix that. The best extras for the bike I bought were the mirrors. They were essential for the Czech Republic where the drivers had no great affection for cyclists and on occasion ran you close to the roadside. It was surprising really since after ice hockey, cycling was their biggest sport. The cycle from Prague to the Austrian border was straightforward for the first 50km. Then for almost two days I experienced hill after hill, 1:8's usually, so it wasn't cycling in the strict sense, more like pushing the bike up a hill and freewheeling down it. I found it hard going and as much as I liked the Czech people, and Prague, I was looking forward to cycling into Austria.

Cynthia blending in well on Plauen Station

Yes, this is a designated cycle path, Czech Republic style

5

THE EARLY DAYS

Time To Go To Sea

At eighteen I was finally able to escape my family and take on the outside world. My career on the Oriana took hold and I started life as a rating, waiting tables. It transpired that a number of the ship's ratings were new and known as 'first trippers. My cabin was a two berth which I shared with a guy called Al Liversedge, who was also a first tripper from Middlesbrough. We became good mates and worked together in the same restaurant on the same station. All of the new crew bonded well. We were from different backgrounds but all broadly of a similar age. My family had been right about a few things; most of the crew were gay, there were drugs a plenty if you wanted them and several ex-cons thrown in the mix for good measure. On a long voyage it was essential to look out for one another. Several times it was necessary to go down to the crew deck and find out why the waiter on the same or next station hadn't turned to. Invariably, it was because of an all-night card school and upon entering the cabin, you frequently had to remove the stoker who was lying on top of the waiter you were trying to 'put on the shake'! There was a real cross section of society. So long as people knew who and what you were, there were very few issues. My first six-and-a-half-month placement flew by.

The work was hard. Apart from the normal restaurant duties, we were on a rota to serve afternoon teas, which nobody liked as most of us wanted to get our head down for a couple of hours in the afternoon. After lunch we were assigned a scrub out where we had to change into grey striped working jackets, which were referred to as piss jackets (although I never understood the derivation of that title). After assembling in the restaurant, one of the assistant head waiters would assign each of us a section. We were given a bucket of warm water, into which was poured some red coloured liquid with the consistency of glue. With a handful of wire wool, we scrubbed the parquet floor until it passed inspection. After dinner service I had to collect the table linen, count and bag it all and take it to the laundry.

At the beginning of the voyage, we were asked to choose a port of call for our day off. We only had one day off, although when we were overnighting in cities like Vancouver or Sydney, we did get time off, as well as the occasional afternoon in some ports. I chose Nassau, which was towards the end of the first trip, and treated myself to a beachside lunch on Providence Island, followed by shark fishing in the afternoon, where I managed to land a 56lb Tiger Shark!

During the day we bronzed on deck, it was a wonderful feeling to have 100 degrees of heat on your back. Little did I realise that fifty years later bits of me would be gradually removed because of the lack of factor 50! Looking over the side, down to the bow cutting through the azure water, I passed many a pleasant hour watching flying fish dodging the ship, together with dolphins who would follow us and play in our wake. The metal deck would become red hot in the sun. As our feet became used to it, we could walk without feeling. It was only when I was on shore leave, that a drawing pin was removed from my foot. I hadn't realised it was there and didn't know how long it had been embedded. Evenings were invariably spent down at The Pig and Whistle; all ships had a crew bar called The Pig and Whistle. We played cards, there were some serious card schools on board. There were also several alcoholics whose consumption defied belief, most of these guys worked in the plate room in the kitchen. It was always a contest to locate a starter in the ice tray and avoid disturbing numerous cans of Tennent's beneath them.

I quickly learned that there was nothing sacred to a merchant seaman. This sentiment was illustrated the evening before docking in Vancouver after a cruise to Honolulu, Acapulco, LA and San Francisco. 'Dropsy Night' was always a time when the waiters smiled broadly, and nothing was too much trouble. It was brown envelope night when said envelopes were passed between passengers or 'bloods' as they were known (since the waiters wanted to bleed them), and hopefully each contained a large gratuity (or 'dropsy' as it was known). It was an evening of high expectation, when waiters attempted to guess what each passenger would give. Envelopes were opened and a mixture of emotions would ensue, from wild surprise to "fucking hell, that's crap, tight bastard"! There were always surprises. This particular evening on my station, which I shared with another pair of waiters, Martha (not his real name) was serving the Pear Belle Helene to a couple. As he placed the dish on the table (and I witnessed this first-hand), the gentleman gave a deep groan, clutched his chest and slipped sedately beneath the table, largely out of sight. His wife naturally enough went into shock and the Ship's Doctor was called. The poor chap was pronounced dead at the scene and his wife was guided away from the restaurant to be comforted. In the kitchen, people were expressing their sympathy to the waiter when Martha turned and said, "Fuck that, there goes my dropsy".

Although Al and I enjoyed our time enormously on the Oriana, our heads were turned arriving in Southampton Water when we passed the newly launched RMS QE2 which was sailing out on sea trials to be followed by her maiden voyage. We had signed up for the next batch of cruises on the Oriana but we both decided to transfer onto the QE2 after they were completed.

The QE2 was out on her maiden voyage when Al and I walked into Cunard House in Southampton to ask for a job. We were told no. They had a long list of reserve crew wanting to join and it would be several months before we were likely to sign on. Undaunted, we both arrived on the doorstep the following morning and every morning after that at 8am before the staff arrived and kept asking the same question. The staff gradually warmed to us over time and began inviting us in to share the first brew of the day. They knew we were staying at The Seaman's Mission and kicking our heels until the next day. Rejection though was not in our vocabulary. After almost three weeks of this, the personnel officer invited us both in and confirmed that we had secured positions as waiters on the QE2 if we wanted to take them! Our diligence had paid off. The QE2 remains in my opinion, the most beautiful liner ever built, a proper ship, unlike the huge flat bellied floating hotels that sail today and can accommodate a small town.

We could not wait to get aboard, initially we had to do our time, working for two trips in the plate wash, before getting the approval to don the red jacket and take our place in the Britannia Restaurant. If anything, the work rate seemed more intensive than on the Oriana. Our day started at 6.30am and rarely finished before midnight, after which we had to wash and iron our kit in readiness for the next day. We were grateful to get a couple of hours sleep during the afternoons, unless we were in port. Regular eating for the crew was almost impossible, so often you would grab what you could. There were many times when I devoured a fillet steak or chicken leg 'on the wing' between leaving the restaurant and taking the escalator down to the kitchen. So much for masticating each mouthful forty times!

It was hard work but financially rewarding. I was not yet twenty and making big bucks. Had I been an old head on young shoulders I would (and should) have invested my money in property. I lived the good life, owning a brand new TR6 sports car cash on the nail. Life on board had its moments, almost universally they were good times but some not so. In the 'not so' category there was a clique of Scouse and Irish crew and at one point there was almost one crew member a night visiting the sick bay. It transpired that amongst this group was an IRA cell. We heard subsequently of IRA threats to blow up the ship in the Mid Atlantic. On one occasion, it was found that on the tender at Cobh, a crate remained unclaimed. We heard that it turned out to be full of machine guns and handguns. Arriving in Southampton, security swarmed the crew quarters and after ripping apart the bulkhead behind our cabin, they apparently found fifty seven grenades and various handguns stored. The cell was arrested that day, and all subsequently received lengthy prison sentences. We also had issues with what purported to be union matters over the 'unfair' sacking of crew. This involved my mate Al, who had begun to go off the rails. His behaviour was precipitated by his girlfriend who declined his offer of marriage. He found solace in smoking weed before graduating to the harder stuff. One evening I returned to the cabin to find him comatose. It transpired that he had hit the LSD and was having a bad trip. The Ship's Doctor told me to turn the lights off and leave him alone, he would come out of it, which he did two days later. As a consequence, he was DR'ed which in shoreside parlance meant he was sacked and would leave the ship on our return to Southampton. His merchant navy career was effectively over.

Al and I shared a waiting station in the restaurant with two others. John was about ten years older than I and had certainly been around the block. We got on well and both of us realised Al was 'going his own way', which wasn't mine. When Al left the ship, John and I worked together and it was the start of a lifetime friendship that endures today.

Times soon turned scary on the QE2. There was a hard core of crew causing trouble and looking for a fight, you didn't want to be in the wrong place at the wrong time. One waiter had turned to, having had an extra bevvy or three, and proceeded to throw soup over a passenger following a disagreement about his order. The union reps on board were a front for mob rule. In a meeting they called in the Britannia Restaurant, virtually all ratings attended following a decision by the Captain to sack around twenty two troublemakers. Only three of us chose to put our hands up to support the decision to sack the offending crew, instead of going on strike. That made us marked men; the three of us were John and I and an elderly waiter. Soon afterwards, I was due to collect the stores from seven deck. Whether John knew or not, and I suspect he got wind something was brewing, I do not know, but he got me to sort the linen while he did the stores run. He was ambushed by five crew on seven deck. Had that been me, I might have got the better of maybe one, possibly two, but I would have taken a real beating. However, John was as strong as an ox and a street fighter. Suffice to say he took all five down, put three in sick bay and in return received a sore rib and a black eye. The situation could not be allowed to continue, it was a reign of fear. The Captain immediately flew home twenty two crew under guard from New York with a double DR in their logbooks, meaning they could never go to sea again. Once that element had been removed, life settled down to a much more enjoyable routine. It was reassuring never having to look over your shoulder again.

When I left the QE2 to travel under my own steam, John remained on board. With the passing of time, we lost touch for many years. Then one fateful day in 1986, I was walking along New George Street in Plymouth when I saw John heading towards the entrance to Debenhams. You cannot miss his very distinctive lope. I called across and from that moment we renewed our friendship. I also had the opportunity to meet his wife, Janet. Fate dealt all four aces in the pack that day, we regularly keep in touch and see each other.

My observation that there was nothing sacred to a merchant seaman proved true on several occasions. One of the waiters who was a real character and always liked a bet took on a challenge to walk around the restaurant during dinner service with his todger out. I can't recall how much the bet was for, but it ran into hundreds of dollars. Being the sportsman that he was, he took the bet. One evening with silver salver in hand, todger laid thereupon, garnished with lettuce and salad, he walked into the restaurant, around his station, and then around the restaurant and back into the kitchen. Not one of the passengers or officers noticed, and he duly collected his winnings and became an overnight sensation.

The winter cruise season was always enjoyable. We were based in New York and regularly had overnight stays, so we got to know the city well. Heading back late at night, after a few drinks or having watched some 'C' rated horror movie on 42nd Street, John and I would often stop off in the all-night diner on 52nd street. It was close to where the QE2 berthed, and we would always bulk up on meatloaf and cheesecake before returning to the ship. While at sea, after finishing serving the evening meal and having laid up for breakfast, we would gather up a few cokes, some ice and a bottle of Bacardi and head for the crew deck area adjacent to the funnel. We'd pour ourselves a couple of large drinks and watch the distant islands pass by while we put the world to rights.

I turned and switched off my alarm clock. Something was amiss; there was no gentle throbbing from the engines and no light. We had sailed for two days out of New York with a full complement of 2,000 passengers heading for St Lucia. I turned to at the appointed hour to be told (with no surprise) that the ship had broken down. It transpired that there was a serious problem which could not be fixed in the short-term. Passengers started to busily discuss whether we would be taken by aliens, as we were adrift in the Bermuda Triangle. All sorts of hypotheses were considered. With no electricity, the kitchens began to heat up quickly which rapidly became a health issue since food could no longer be kept refrigerated. Fortunately, the Sea Venture cruise ship soon honed into view. All passengers were transferred by tender, in calm conditions, and taken to Bermuda, the nearest port. We waited for a tug to arrive from New York, which also towed us to Bermuda. There we waited several days while repairs were carried out and we took full advantage of the free time in port. The Robin Hood Club in Hamilton took some money that week!

I worked in the restaurant for two years before I changed tack and became a bedroom steward, swapping the red jacket for green. Again, I began at the bottom and started with thirteen cabins on five deck. The routine suited me well, though I continued to work long hours. It wasn't quite the sixteen-hour-day I'd had in the restaurant, but it was still well into double figures. I enjoyed the greater sense of independence. Of course there were regular Captain's inspections, but it was an opportunity to get to know the passengers on a one-to-one basis. I certainly saw another side to our guests! I served morning tea or breakfast on more than one occasion where a lady would open the cabin door completely naked and be happy to remain so while I deposited the tray. Dressed for dinner, they looked a million dollars, some were drop dead gorgeous. Then reality would kick in as I entered their stateroom to tidy and present the room for when they returned to retire. Some rooms looked like a bomb had hit them, with clothes everywhere and knickers all over the place. By the time I had finished and closed the stateroom door, the bathrooms were clean with fresh towels, the room was tidy with everything folded and put away, the bed was turned down with the lady's negligee carefully arranged on top and low lighting was turned on with a chocolate placed on the pillow.

I spent five wonderful years in the Merchant Navy, during which time I travelled extensively and experienced some fascinating cultures and places. To many it would have been sufficient to satisfy a wanderlust, but not me. Virtually all the places I visited had been on the coast, I had not seriously ventured inland and explored what countries were really like. My career path could, however, have been so different had fate not stepped in.

I loved the life at sea, and I was beginning to think about developing a career path. Many of the guys on the boat were happy to remain where they were as the money was so good. The tips were astronomical and many of the waiters and bedroom stewards invested wisely in property over the years, some owned quite a portfolio. I had been thinking about becoming an officer although I was aware I did not have the academic qualifications. Nevertheless, I wrote on the off chance to Cunard House and was asked to attend an interview in Southampton when we next docked. At that time Cunard had three liners; the QE2, the Cunard Adventurer, and the Cunard Ambassador, which had just been built. The lack of qualifications was balanced out by my 'hands on' experience at sea and with the company. Shortly after the interview I was informed that I was under consideration for junior purser aboard the Cunard Ambassador, which was undergoing a positioning trip between Port Everglades and New Orleans at the time. She was to be based in Miami where she would operate a cruise programme around the Caribbean. I immediately accepted. I was advised that I could not remain on the QE2 as it would be difficult making the transition from rating to officer on the same ship. At the time we had just sailed from New York and were heading home. A day later I was called into the Chief Purser's Office to be advised that the Cunard Ambassador had caught fire off the Florida Keys and was severely damaged. Consequently, there was no possibility that I would be joining the ship. Thus, ended my seagoing career before it had begun. The Cunard Ambassador was never reprieved, her hull was sold, and her fate was to become a sheep carrier in the Baltic!

First trip and port - SS Oriana in Lisbon

A lot of the crew bought property; I bought a Spitfire!

6

AND SO WE MOVE ON

Cycling the Danube

As I crossed the border from the Czech Republic into Austria, I could not help but notice the contrast between the two countries. Austria immediately felt unshackled by a history of former Soviet influence. It had great cycling, excellent roads, and directional signage. The countryside was beautiful, a real patchwork, of course I was on the lowland belt so cycling proved to be much easier. The villages were attractive, immaculately maintained, with an assortment of different coloured houses, varied architecture and a common feature for most was a small church that sat in the village square. Looking back, Austria provided perfect cycling conditions for weather, topography and scenery. I camped in orchards, with the tent frequently hidden in the long grass. One night I slept in a wild cherry orchard and watched the sunrise, which was beautiful. It was a pleasure waking every morning with the sun on the tent and the warmth on my body. I cycled in shorts and a tee shirt with a constant temperature of around 23°C, it was perfect.

It was easy cycling throughout Austria, and I averaged over 100km a day; my best distance was 117km and in total I had completed around 2,000km. My next stop was Vienna and after that I planned to continue cycling along the Danube, which was a very popular European cycle route, through to Bratislava and onto Budapest.

I had started to meet an increasing number of cyclists along my route, and people generally became less reticent to ask where I was from or what I was doing. Upon arriving in Vienna, I made my way to the Tourist Information Office and picked up suggestions for a tour and what to see by bicycle. As I set off on Cynthia, I looked up and saw a Starbucks. I remember thinking 'so, there is a God!'. I studied the literature over a large coffee and double chocolate muffin and managed to locate a suitable hostel in the city centre. I stayed in Vienna for three days and thought it was beautiful. Schönbrunn Palace was simply magnificent, however the city itself was swarming with tourists. I much preferred Prague, although smaller, it had a stronger character and I felt more at home in its labyrinth of pedestrian areas.

At the end of my stay, I picked up the cycle route that led to Budapest on the other side of the Danube. Initially, I followed the river, observing the naturist sun worshippers for several kilometres, which in some instances was a pleasant distraction. I then lost the river heading inland and around two hours later I came across Henri's Cafe and Bar, which sat directly on the cycle route. Looking at the customers' waistlines, I guessed that many were very recreational cyclists (at a stretch). I went looking for a coke, but for twice the quantity and 20p more I could get a beer, there was no contest. The beer slipped down well, and I continued along an excellent cycle path picking up the Danube close to Bratislava. The Danube was wide, more so than the Tamar, and it certainly wasn't blue, not by any stretch. It was more like the swirling muddy morass of the River Parrett, which flowed through my childhood home of Bridgwater. It wasn't the most scenic piece of river at this juncture.

Bratislava was only 67km from Vienna, it was a decent morning's ride and I arrived just around lunch. It was another beautiful city, similar in many respects to Prague although much smaller. Like Prague, it displayed wonderful architecture around the central historical quarter.

On leaving Bratislava I continued to follow the Danube, which formed the extension of cycleway 6 (the route extended from the source of the river in Germany to its mouth on the Black Sea). On my way, I ran into a group of seventeen Brits from London who were doing a cycle trip between Bavaria and Budapest. This was something they arranged annually for fun in different European locations. What a bunch they were, everyone to the man was so interesting and ready to chat. The group had a history too, one member had raised just under a million pounds for charity from his cycle rides. Many of the others were raising money for the Norwood Trust, which helped people with handicaps. Invariably their cash was raised from cycle tours and their next venue was Sri Lanka. I had a great day riding with these fellers, and they kindly donated to my own charity, Children with Cancer UK, by thrusting notes into my pocket after dinner! I was very grateful to them all, and it was such a highlight to bump into them.

Up until that point, meeting long distance cyclists had been rarer than hen's teeth. Whilst quietly cycling along the Danube I came across a dozen or so Croats who were cycling from Zagreb to London. I stopped to say hello and they swarmed around me with their cameras out. I wasn't sure how my reputation had spread quite so far so quickly, but I was soon brought down to reality. It was Cynthia who was drawing all the admiring glances! She drew a cacophony of comments; "it's a Thorn", "wow, never seen one of these", "steel is real" (a catch phrase used in the company's literature). She certainly got all the treatment. They thought the nomad was the greatest bike on the planet, but Cynthia was the first they had seen in the flesh.

After wild camping along the riverbank, I laid up short of Budapest in a campsite and made my way into the city the following morning. The city unfolded before me as the river meandered through. The vista was sublime and as I approached the city, I cycled alongside waterfront housing and quaint cafes. I decided to stay for two nights at the Wombat hostel, which gave me time to explore the city and plan my ongoing route.

I stayed in Budapest a little longer than anticipated. This was because the fourth and little finger on my right hand became fixed at around ninety degrees to the rest of my fingers. They didn't hurt but looked strange. I investigated the condition and found that it was quite common with cyclists; the remedy was to see a physio. With the help of the reception at the hostel I found one, a delightful lady, who specialised in sports injuries and who applied treatment using a combination of ultrasound and a massage gun. She assured me my fingers would gradually return to normal, and they did. I loved the atmosphere in Budapest, and by the end of my stay it had become one of my favourite cities.

Initially I had planned to follow the Danube down to Belgrade and across the Balkans to northern Greece. After some research it became clear that there would be little advantage in going that route. The topography looked mountainous and I'd heard there was little scenic value, there were no campsites and wild camping was prohibited in Croatia and Serbia due to land mines. I was not particularly taken with the idea of Romania, so I decided to backtrack by heading to Venice by train. From there I planned to cycle along the Adriatic coast to Brindisi, where I would catch a ferry to Greece. I contemplated exploring the possibility of finding a ferry service that could take me from Greece to

Cyprus and on to Egypt, Jordan, Israel, or Lebanon, but there didn't seem to be any, so I gave up on that idea and decided to cycle across to Turkey instead.

The thirteen hour train ride departed from Budapest and stopped off in Vienna and Salzburg before Innsbruck, where I would have to change to catch the connection to Verona. It was an evening departure and loading the bike onto the train proved quite an effort since the carriages were about three feet higher than the platform; Cynthia wasn't exactly user friendly in that regard. Assistance came in the form of a feller called Harith who lived in London and who had himself cycled out to Budapest, but in about a quarter of the time it had taken me. He had a road bike with two panniers with a total weight of ten kilos. Being a fit 21-year-old, used to the cycling rigours of London, he was averaging 200km a day! 'Some feat that,' I thought, 'oh to be twenty-one'. Harith was excellent company and was heading to Zurich and back to London.

I arrived in Innsbruck at 4am and had a five hour wait for the connection. I managed a brief nap in the waiting room before chatting to a security guy who very kindly opened the lost and found office so that I could store the bike in safety. I then watched the sun rise over the Alps, the town was surrounded by jagged peaks and there was a clear view of a ski jump from the station. The rail journey through the Alps was truly something, the Alps formed a stunning backdrop although I was extremely glad that I didn't have to cycle over them.

The train pulled into Verona in the middle of the afternoon. The city was simply magnificent. Despite having a personal dislike of opera, the city still had that something that grabbed me. The focal point was the Arena, which was fronted at one point by three sphinxes covered in hieroglyphics. Close by was the Tourist Information Centre, which had invariably become my first port of call. I queued in the accommodation line only to be addressed by the assistant who, when I asked if there was a hostel for around twenty euros in the vicinity, gave me a full on Italian glare. "We only deal with hotels here" came the curt reply, as her eyes cast bolts of fire towards the image of my oil stained shorts, a sweat stained tee shirt and a linen scarf around my neck. I was not exactly dressed to kill, I will concede, but there I was, and if she could have driven me out of the city limits then and there, I think she would have. "So, I take it, that's a no then?" I replied. Fortunately, a young assistant was watching and spoke perfect English. She invited me over with her finger and produced a street map to direct me to the one hostel in Verona, as well as a campsite as an alternative. She even knew what they all charged! There is a lot to be said for finding the right queue the first time around.

The hostel was a former villa and architecturally magnificent. The ablutions were Neolithic, built of stone and incredible. I had never stayed in a 36-bed dorm before nor had I stayed in a hostel where the rules were so many, down to what you could eat for breakfast! Still, it did not bother me. In the evening I walked around the city, its affluence was staggering. The restaurants surrounding one half of the Arena were doing a brisk trade with diners of all nationalities who were waiting for the gates to open and the opera to begin. I quickly realised in Italy to never sit down at a table with a cloth, especially if laid, as it was expensive. I learnt to avoid waiters dressed in a waistcoat for the same reason. It was a real pleasure walking around the narrow streets with all the branded shop names.

The following day I took the train to Venice for the day. I set off early and arrived mid-morning. Exiting Venice SL (Santa Lucia) Station was certainly a contrast to Paddington Station. It was quite simply surreal. The station opened up to a vista of canals and stunning waterfront architecture. I carefully avoided the tour operators and walked through the streets to the Rialto Bridge and St Mark's Square. I kept going after that. Every corner, every turn was just wonderful, with narrow streets, restaurants and shops. I spent a few minutes watching cargo boats being unloaded (the water equivalent of Parcel Force), with goods transferred onto large trollies. I saw one boat decked out in its international livery of yellow and orange. Fortunately, the narrow streets were not overcrowded so it was easy to keep moving. I decided on lunch, well it was that or a gondola ride and as I was on my own it didn't seem quite the thing. I also went on the lookout for a polyester football shirt, not cotton, as I needed something quick drying that would retain its shape through constant sweating. The choice of shirts was good. I quickly discounted those with Rooney on the back but considered Messi. I bypassed the array of Italian shirts and the French shirts did not even get a look in. Strangely, they did not have a Plymouth Argyle shirt (I was a proud owner of one, and carried it with me), so I settled eventually on a tasteful Chelsea home shirt with Torres emblazoned on the back. I had never been to Venice before, and it was worth every second.

I stayed in Verona for two nights, planning my route and taking in the city. If I had had the right bank balance, I could have spent quite a bit of time there. The lady who managed the hostel, who hitherto had appeared somewhat direct, was extremely sweet when I asked for directions out of town! One thing a cyclist needs to know about Italy, is where you can cycle (I will not say safely, not with the way the Italians drive) and where you must avoid. Only someone from another planet would contemplate trying to cycle on the autostrada, which was definitely off limits along with dual carriageways and city exits and entrances. I constantly had problems in these areas. Luckily, this lady knew her stuff and put me right onto a minor road. I was full of ice cream and raring to go. Perfect weather conditions meant that I made the Adriatic Coast by early evening with a personal best of 183km for the day. I promptly managed to find a campsite and staggered into the tent to sleep. In my exhausted state I would have paid anything, on this occasion it was twenty-two euros. Italy, whilst beautiful, was not cheap and all the way through, the thing that really bugged me was that I had to pay the same as a motor home, or a six man tent, just to be squashed into an area that wasn't that big. I wild camped whenever I could. A lot of the sites were jam packed full, but as with any seasonal location, the summer was where these places made their money. I tried the old soldier routine, but it never met with much success.

The next morning, I cycled down the coast to a city called Ravenna. Now for cyclists, this place was as close to a black hole as you could get; once in never out! Throughout Italy I cycled on or by the SS16, which was essentially the coast road. There was no chance of cycling out of Ravenna on this route though, as it was a dual carriageway. While people tried to help with directions, I quickly realised that I was going nowhere. I ended up on a minor road to Bologna and did an exceptionally large circuitous route to Cervia on the coast. Despite my mileage the day before, the distance on this day, although significant, meant that I had not travelled all that far.

I had seen hideous pictures of Rimini in the 1970s when it had matched Benidorm as the grot resort of Europe. This is no longer the case and I was impressed with the city. Yes, it was what it was, but it was so much better than I had envisaged, with new hotels that reminded me of

Bournemouth. It was an exhilarating feeling cycling along this part of the coast, next to the Adriatic. In the heat I estimated I was consuming between ten and twelve litres of liquid a day, hardly anything touched the sides, it went straight down. The water in my bottles became warm in 10 minutes, literally, so it was in cafes or supermarkets where I tanked up.

Over the next few days, I visited Pesaro, Ancona, Pescara, and a beautiful town called Termoli. I was struck down with a bug, so on one occasion I frog hopped on the train where the topography was steep or decidedly uninteresting around the peninsula close to Foggia. I suppose in all, I lost around 120-140km. The one thing I will say about Italian trains is that they were cheap. I was also able to get off and continue my journey the following day on different trains if I could. I loved the sheer abandonment Italians displayed when seeing each other or saying goodbye. No other place on earth would I have seen a conductor needing to walk half the platform to invite a couple in passionate embrace (one on the train, the other on the platform) to separate, so that he could close the doors and get the train moving! With a bicycle I was restricted to local services, but that was fine. There was still the problem of lifting Cynthia several feet into the air onto the train, and reversing the process getting off. Invariably someone would help me, even the driver! I thought the Italians were wonderful, so friendly and ready to help whenever possible. I found their expressive ways so amusing. Why say something that only your friends will hear when you can tell the whole street! The hand and arm expressions to go with the vocalisation also worked a treat. Like Europeans generally, the Italians smoked like chimneys. Now, I had no problem with this, I never minded having a beer with a waft of smoke in the air. It may make medical sense not to smoke and treat people who do like a pariah (as the nanny state in the UK does), but I'm all for freedom of choice.

The night before arriving in Bari I stayed on a site in Bisceglie. What another gem of a place it was. I opened my tent flap with the Adriatic right beside me. I couldn't figure out why the site was half empty, given the facilities included UK style loos. The old French style 'stand and deliver' that were prevalent in the 1960s in France, were still common in some sites on the way down through Italy. Well, I found out soon enough, next door was a night club and opposite, was a hotel. Overnight, a battle raged in decibel count as to which venue could make the most noise. I think the club did, finishing at a very respectable 5.30am! I was always up at, or before, 7am anyway as the tent became a sauna after that. The other campers and I trooped out the following morning (I had intended to anyway) and I felt sorry for the owner's daughter who was somewhat upset and invited me to stay for an extra night at the same rate. I assume she had little success with those who preceded me, since nobody did a U-turn. As I cycled into Bari, I was again prevented from continuing along the dreaded SS16 and I had to drag Cynthia across scrubland, along a dirt track, and through a dry riverbed to get to the road that would eventually lead me to the port.

One of us made it ok!

A refreshing early morning beer by the Danube

Entering Budapest

Perfect cycling along the Adriatic coast

7

THE EARLY DAYS

To Africa And Beyond

After having left the Merchant Navy, I still had no idea what I wanted to do with my life or career. All I had was this inexhaustible thirst for travel which would not go away. I think like many, the thirst for travel was part of a journey to find my place in the world whether it be by happenstance or fate. I stayed at home briefly, examining my options. Life at home wasn't great, I dipped in and out of a few jobs and I was annoyed and frustrated with myself for not knowing what I should be doing. I knew that staying at home was not the answer. Dad had retired early from the bank, having had a nervous breakdown. I did not feel comfortable in the home environment and I was mindful that I had to seek pastures new, so I sold my car and decided to try my luck abroad. I bought a ticket to Johannesburg and headed to Heathrow. It was 1973 and apartheid was in full flow so I had no real reason to pick South Africa over Australia or anywhere else. I collected my rucksack and made my way through customs. An officer invited me into an office and asked me a few questions concerning my visit. I had no idea how long I was going to stay. I had a one-way ticket and no immediate plans to return to England. The officer passed me some papers adding that if I wished, and signed the papers presented, I could become a South African citizen overnight. I declined, feeling that it would be a sensible option to look around first and see if citizenship was what I wanted. He was fine with that and so I went on my way.

I knew nobody in South Africa. I was told that I had some distant relatives in Benoni, near Johannesburg, who were involved in the diamond business. However, after looking them up, they made it clear that they did not wish to develop any long lost cousin relationships or have anything to do with me for any longer than they had to. So, I decided, as winter was approaching, to head to Durban and look for work. I began hitchhiking and having made my way out of the city, I got a lift from a guy and his mate in a pickup who were heading towards Durban. I slung my gear in the back and jumped in as well. Driving across the Drakensberg I almost froze. Having put on every bit of clothing I had, I crouched down away from the icy wind that was blowing across the Transvaal. Eventually, I reached Durban and booked into a hostel. I quickly found out that the easiest place to find employment was with South African Railways (SAR). I found their offices, and after submitting an application I began working as a forklift truck driver in the Port of Durban. The port operated a clear delineation of duties. Casual labour like myself tended to drive the forklifts, we collected freight on pallets from the ship and dispensed it into one of the sheds along the quayside. I found that most of the guys driving forklifts were like myself, earning a bit of money then moving on. The admin and paperwork roles were undertaken by the Afrikaners, who were in general very officious and a complete contrast to us on the forklifts. The hard labour, which involved sorting the pallets and moving goods in the shed, was carried out by black South Africans. The Afrikaners treated the black workers with disdain, the forklift drivers felt much the same towards the Afrikaners and so the relationship between us drivers and the hard labourers was pretty good.

On one occasion, a black foreman was standing on a pallet and was being hoisted over the ship, above the grain hold, when he tumbled and fell in headfirst. He was pulled out and hoisted again from the ship onto the quay, where he sat down against the shed. It was only then that I realised his 'safety' helmet was embedded in his head. He said he was ok and eventually wandered off. In another incident, I was loading pallets onto a railway truck with the help of an African labourer. As he was piling the goods to one end, his foot slipped, the side of the truck opened and trapped his ankle, virtually severing it. Immediately I switched the forklift off and ran to his aide. His ankle was literally hanging on by a thread. He didn't shout or anything. I stripped off my tee shirt and made a tourniquet which I tied above his knee. It wasn't a pretty sight, there was blood everywhere. I shouted to the Afrikaans Foreman, who was in charge of the shed we were operating in, to get an ambulance. He wanted to know what colour the injured person was. "Fucking orange and what the fuck has that got to do with anything!" I yelled back in disbelief. The ambulance took twenty minutes to arrive. It was that incident, along with several other observations, that made me realise South Africa wasn't for me and if the customs officer I had met in the airport on my way in was to ask the same question again, it would have been a decisive no. Having spent nine months in South Africa, I decided to move on and see a bit more of Africa.

There was no state-of-the-art hiking gear in the 70s, or designer outdoor shops where you could buy the latest kit, you just used everyday clothing. I sorted my rucksack, purchased some new tee shirts and a map of the African Continent, and began to hitchhike through Africa. In those days everyone hitchhiked in England, Europe and all around the world. I always picked up hitchhikers, mostly students but travellers as well. Invariably they were great company, and I passed many an hour listening to their stories. I was always grateful to be picked up myself. I had some stimulating conversations and found it incredible how kind and helpful people could be and were, always willing to go the extra mile or two to make sure I got to where I was going safely. It's not something you see these days, unfortunately we have developed this snowflake approach to life which has become ever more endemic throughout our society. Of course, there was always a risk, particularly for girls, but you usually had a good idea of when to stop and when not to.

Heading north of Durban, I travelled through Rhodesia (Zimbabwe as it now is), Zambia, Tanzania, Kenya and Egypt. Rhodesia was a beautiful country, it had an almost perfect climate, a vibrant agricultural industry, and I think uniquely something like 97 of the then 103 minerals in the periodic table could be found there. Rhodesia boasted huge tin and coal reserves. Apartheid did not appear to be quite so obvious either, as public transport and many public facilities permitted black and white folk together, unlike South Africa, where it was always segregated. Tourism was also a major industry, with the wildlife, Lake Kariba (the world's largest man-made lake), and of course the jewel in the crown, Victoria Falls, which was twice the height of Niagara. I managed to get a holiday job for a couple of months based at the Victoria Falls Hotel, taking groups of visitors around the landmark. I never tired of the views, which were awe inspiring and the sunsets over the Zambezi River were simply stunning. In my opinion, Victoria Falls are the most beautiful of all the major falls around the world.

As I progressed through Africa, it was quite usual to spend several days in the bush with very few cars passing. I would sit by the side of the road when, quite frequently, there would be a distraction or noise, as the vegetation became disturbed. I watched as elephants and gazelles crossed the road, sometimes more worryingly a troop of baboons. Raising a tent near a village at sunset was a curious experience for the local inhabitants, who were always inquisitive and friendly, so much so that the children would gather around and watch me as I boiled water to make tea. I was invited to stay in villages in Tanzania and Kenya. The villagers were extremely poor but proud and took it as an honour that I would wish to stay with them. They provided food, usually watermelon and a maize based mash, as well as something resembling a stew that included chunks of meat (which from my expanding lexicon of Swahili, was dog or some form of rodent). At one point my digestive system gave way, and I collapsed on a main street in Mombasa with a temperature of 105 degrees and a body covered in yellow puss-like spots. Fortunately, this incident occurred near a pharmacy. The Asian pharmacist diagnosed my condition on the spot and fed me all sorts of potions before further dosing me up and arranging for me to recover in a hotel. What was not clear at the time, although I wasn't in much state to appreciate my surroundings (other than where the nearest facilities were), was that the hotel was a brothel! Quiet it was not, and the occupants were in no frame of mind to sympathise with my condition. I visited the pharmacist to thank him five days later, and he once again dosed me up insisting that I take everything he supplied. On my way back to the hotel, I purchased a large padlock. For some reason, all the rooms could be padlocked from the outside! I had no idea why. Since the young ladies next door had given me such a hard time and were clearly enjoying themselves, as a parting gift, I carefully slipped the padlock through the rings and snapped it shut taking the keys with me. All the rooms had a tiny mesh covered window, which no adult could climb through, so how long they remained inside, and whether the incumbent seamen managed to re-join their ship before sailing, I could not say.

I had many amazing experiences in Africa, as well as Victoria Falls, trekking through banana groves up to the two lower levels of Mt Kilimanjaro, 9,000ft and 12,000ft respectively, was a real highlight (I didn't possess the correct footwear to make it to the summit). At first base, the accommodation was comprised of a couple of huts with bunks and basic cooking facilities. At dawn, cloud cover extended over the rift valley below. Adjacent to the huts was a rain forest with carpets of purple flowers. The views were breath-taking, so I decided to stay another day and explore the rainforest and the mountain.

I met some fascinating people on the road; a Belgium Baron and his wife who worked for an international development organisation and a couple from Somerset. He was a mining engineer and while staying with them for a couple of days, I was taken down a copper mine in Zambia. It was over a kilometre underground and only accessible by a shaft lift.

It wasn't all beer and skittles, however. I found myself in jail twice, the first time was due to inaccurate directions. I managed to climb into a jail yard in Tanzania and was quickly escorted through the compound by two friendly guards down the hillside and to the road below, where I continued hitchhiking. I never imagined inmates wore the uniform with arrows so commonly depicted in old films, but they did, and they cheered loudly as I was escorted between them; it was a surreal experience. The second time happened in Cairo. I was incarcerated for five days because of the expiry of my yellow fever inoculation. Whilst inside, I met up with an Egyptian chap who was roughly my age and whose family were wealthy. His father owned one of the most prestigious bazaars and, as the large photograph in their lounge testified, had proudly escorted Princess Margaret around it when she visited in the 1960s. He had the situation well under control. Every evening the guards were bribed, so we slipped over the wall at around 7pm under the cover of darkness and were met and driven away by his brothers in their Mercedes to the family home. We ate supper with the rest of his family, then went onto Memphis and the night clubs, before heading back to the jail, making it over the wall in time for roll call at 6am and back to our cells for the day. My passport was eventually returned and I was booked onto the first flight to Europe, which happened to be Athens. This was good news as I had friends there. Rather than turn left for England, I decided to turn right and head for Asia.

In the 70s, the Magic Bus was a well-known and popular way of travelling between the UK and India. It was very much part of the hippy trail and that suited me fine, so I climbed aboard and settled in my seat to İstanbul. The bus took us through Turkey, Iran, Afghanistan, Pakistan and India. In those days the Shah was on the throne and Afghanistan was also more liberal. The girls wore short skirts and the whole outlook was western. Tehran could easily have been Paris or Buenos Aires. It was clear however, that the older generation did not approve of the western influence. During the trip I became mates with a South African of Pakistani origin. Again, comparable in age, we got on extraordinarily well sharing the journey and playing countless and continuous games of chess. I learned a lot about the Muslim faith, and adherence to it, although he was not what I would call resolutely devout. Having a Pakistani passport, he was refused entry into India so we reluctantly said our farewells at the border.

I headed initially to Amritsar and the magnificent Golden Temple and eventually made my way to Kashmir and Dal Lake. Much of the union state of Jammu and Kashmir was a war zone, forming disputed territory between India and

Pakistan. Whilst full of military personnel, the area was beautiful with the Himalayas forming a backdrop along with the K2, the second highest mountain in the world. Srinagar was the summer state capital and it looked like a medieval city, enhanced with examples of its riverfront vernacular architecture incorporated into cantilevered balconies. There was no drainage of course, so I quickly learnt to stay beneath the cantilevers! The city's Mughal gardens were extensive and beautifully laid out. Although early winter was a bleak time of year, there was a haunting beauty across Dal Lake. Following in the wake of other tourists, I rented a houseboat for a couple of weeks. During my stay, I was visited incessantly by local jewellery vendors, who rowed out to the houseboats in small crafts to sell their wares, which were mainly fake of course. Despite resting, I became run down after several months on the road and contracted the usual Indian ailments together with glaucoma. I decided that with winter closing in, it was time to head home. The cheapest flight took me via Damascus where I had to change planes. My intention was to explore the city in the several hours available in between, however, my plans were unfortunately dashed. Going through customs I was taken to one side and searched. The knife which I carried fastened to my leg (security was lax in those days) was confiscated and after strip searching me, I found myself once again in a cell. Apparently, I had been mistaken for an Israeli. Unfortunately my circumcision at birth did not help persuade the local constabulary otherwise. Not long after I had settled into my cell, I received a visit from a gentleman who I took to be a junior representative from the British Embassy. He was clearly ex-public school, and in his mind superior in every way to the likes of his fellow subjects. He looked distinctly hacked off. I reckon I must have disrupted his gin party at the Ambassador's residence or some such. Whatever agreement was struck, I was told that I would remain in the cell overnight and be escorted onto an Egypt Air flight to London the following day.

8

AND SO WE MOVE ON

Jobsworths, Wild Dogs and Terrible Drivers

The ferry to Greece departed Bari in Italy at 8pm, and after stops in Corfu and Igoumenitsa, I arrived in Patras the next day at 1pm. I managed to find a quiet hostel with only one other guest. Close by there was an excellent bike shop and I decided to invest in a saddle cover, since, although my Brookes saddle was well worn in, when I went over any uneven stretches, the rivets did their best to embed themselves into my backside! I stayed in Patras for two nights. It was the end of a heatwave, so it felt sensible to see that out before hitting the trail. My plan was to head up the coast to Delphi, Lamia, Larissa and Thessaloniki before crossing into İstanbul. Greece was cheaper than Italy, which was good news, but the weather was excruciatingly hot and soared to temperatures of 40°C and above. I factored in early morning starts to avoid the sun.

I left Patras at 3am, which gave me time to cover some mileage before the sun rose and allowed me to get across the bridge before the lorries disembarked from the morning ferry. My plans were partially stopped in their tracks by a rather charming Finnish lady whom I met on the hostel steps as I was loading the bike. It transpired that she had come down from Helsinki to try and help her daughter, who lived in Patras and was a heroin addict. It came to light that the daughter had a three-year-old who lived with her grandmother in Finland. Trying to straighten out a teenager or twenty-year-old can be difficult at the best of times, without additional complications. We chatted on the steps, well, I listened. There was very little I could contribute.

I cycled away from the hostel at 4am and made reasonable time across the bridge and onto Itea. I found a family owned campsite at the end of the town and after saying I would rather spend my euros with them, they cooked up a superb moussaka with salad. I didn't realise until too late that it was part of the family meal and I felt very guilty when I found out. Such was the kindness I met along the way in Greece. The following day, I cycled across two mountain ranges to Lamia. I had to push Cynthia the best part of 5km up the first section which was testing. Then, by chance, a pickup pulled in and offered me a lift of 8km to where he was turning off. That 8km took me over the summit, and I reckon it saved me the best part of two hours of the day (such is the way we cyclists think when attempting to get from A to B). The scenery was quite something, the first range opened up to a plateau which was great to cycle around. By 2pm I had made it to Lamia and after an hour's stop, I skirted around the city to a campsite about 20km further on by the sea. Between the city and the campsite lay an industrial area. There were a lot of factories and warehouses, all recently built but vacant, except for roughly 10%. It was a reminder of the difficulties Greece was facing and was a scene that repeated itself throughout several towns and cities. As I passed through villages, the cafes and tavernas were frequented by men with seemingly nothing to do but smoke (the national pastime) and play cards. They strove to make a coffee and water last as long as possible.

The roads in Greece were not cycle friendly. For much of the route I rode on the motorway since it was the only game in town, so to speak. All the locals had said to go ahead, so armed with this knowledge, I did. The main route between Athens and Thessaloniki was a joy to ride, a dual carriageway with a side apron of almost eight feet which I kept within. There was no way I would have cycled on such roads in Italy, but Greece had virtually no traffic during the day and I was not in anyone's way. In comparison, I had seen more traffic on the M5 at Cullompton at 2am! Again, perhaps it was indicative of the country's state of affairs. As well as the lack of freight, there were very few tourists on mainland roads. Between Patras and Thessaloniki, I counted a couple of German plates and a handful of Dutch, that was it. It seemed that most tourists headed for the Islands for two weeks of sex, sand and sea, which was fair enough, but I still couldn't believe how few I came across.

All was quiet on the motorway. I was humming a Coldplay song when a toll station honed into view. I waved and got called over. I saw the price was 1.80 euros for a motorbike and wondered what they would charge me for Cynthia. By the tone of the operative, he sounded like a traffic warden. A couple of sentences later my worst fears were confirmed, he was the ultimate jobsworth in a mild panic. He had obviously never seen a bike on a motorway before and gesticulated for me to get off. "But where?" I asked. He was confused, meanwhile a young Greek feller with an attractive female passenger beside him put the horn on me. It was not a good call on his behalf. I turned slowly, pointed my finger, and waggled it at him, requesting him to be patient. I turned back to the jobsworth who told me to leave the motorway a kilometre distant. He wasn't interested where the road went to, or where I had to get to, he just wanted me out of his jurisdiction. The horn sounded again, accompanied by an arm movement that translated as 'get on with it!'. I got off Cynthia and, having taken something of a dislike to this person in the car, started walking towards him. Jobsworth then shouted and waved me through. I remounted Cynthia (which wasn't easy on a full load!) and set off though the barrier. Unfortunately, he hadn't lifted the gate, so I whipped around the side, setting off all the alarms. I just kept going and picked up on where I had got to with my tune.

Some 40-50km further up the motorway (of course I didn't turn off) I noted a motorway patrol behind me, they followed for a bit, so I pulled in and they drew alongside. The traditional good day greetings in Greek were expressed and fortunately the guy could speak perfect English. He explained that cyclists shouldn't use the motorway and I replied that it was the only route that led to where I needed to go and if he knew of an alternative, I would take it. He rang his mate and then basically told me to get off at the next turn since his boss was 20km behind. If I didn't get off the road, his arse would be on the line. I fully understood the dilemma, and knew the man realised that common sense indicated I should continue, but as he said, "rules are rules". He guided me off and sent me 30km to Volos, where he suggested I should stay for the night. We parted in a very friendly manner and of course he recognised that for where I needed to go, the following day I would return to the motorway. Volos had a vibrant and beautiful waterfront, it was easy to see why it was a popular tourist spot.

The following day, true to form, I was back on the motorway, this time with no problems. It was safer to cycle on the motorway for a myriad of reasons, the A roads near towns were busier, bus drivers were a nightmare as were individuals who suddenly opened their car door not looking or anticipating a cyclist! The road surfaces were badly maintained with potholes, uneven surfaces, and tarmac mounds everywhere. The real problem cycling in Greece however was dogs! They were a major problem from just about every angle. Greece was the first European country where I experienced being chased by dogs. Fortunately, I was on a downslope when I faced a real risk of being bitten and was able to outrun them. Another incident occurred when an overtaking car saw a large feral dog in the road and deliberately swerved towards it to get it out the way, allowing me safe passage. In a village on the way into Thessaloniki, a dog leapt up and chased me. It forgot it was on a lead and was physically pulled back in the air when the lead ran out. I came across a Dutch family whose youngest daughter had been attacked by a dog and it had put them off returning. Put into perspective, Greece faced many acute financial and economic challenges that surpassed anything else, but there was no doubt that the dog issue needed addressing, in order for tourism to grow. I carried a few stones in my pocket and had a cycle security steel rope with a padlock on the end that I could take out and whirl like a mace. I would not have hesitated to use any method to protect myself and would unhesitatingly have sought retribution on any dog that attacked me. I expected to get bitten at some point and went to the locals for advice. Their counsel was unanimous; "stop the bike", "don't swerve into the road where you might get hit by a car", "take the bite if you have to" and "kick the shit out of them". It got to the stage where I was constantly looking around for dogs and it did take away the enjoyment of travelling through the country.

I thought I'd had my fill of jobsworths, but while parked up in a garage about 20km from Volos I was proved wrong. I was relaxing in the shade, when suddenly a policeman walked by. He discharged his bag on the adjoining table and turned around to inspect Cynthia. I said nothing, expecting the usual friendly enquiry asking where I was from but no, this constable looked at me and pointed, saying "Rear light!"

I responded, "Yes and?"

"You have one and it's not on", came the reply, in a tone that suggested I was about to heist the garage. I sensed that this chap had either been the subject of bullying at school or had only ever made the grade as a milk monitor.

I replied, somewhat confused, "Well if you look, I have three rear lights," getting up to point them out, "plus a front light and 8 reflectors on the panniers. I haven't got them on as I'm parked and it's 3.30pm with a full on sun".

I was met with no answer, I began to mildly panic at his rapier-like grasp of my explanation. His ability to sum up a situation whilst demonstrating a complete lack of credible thought was worrying, since he had his hand on his gun (which hitherto had remained holstered). I could not believe the matter was a shooting offence! Fortunately, his mate then rolled up in a squad car and without any acknowledgement he got in and drove off. Surreal!

Thessaloniki was the second largest city in Greece, it was a major tourist hub that linked with many of the islands as it had a commercial port. I arrived at 4pm and immediately went in search of the city centre. A star of a policeman directed me to the Tourist Information Office, but I quickly discovered that it was closed. Closer observation confirmed that since it was a Saturday, the office had shut at 3pm and would remain so until 9am Monday. 'Well, that's just great', I thought! But unlike other travellers, I'm extremely fortunate, I have a Liz. Every traveller wants and needs a Liz. Liz is my sister, a real gem in every way. I texted her and within minutes she had replied with a list of budget places to stay. I was worry free once more.

In the evening, I took a walk along the seafront. It was pleasant but no Portofino, Nice or Cannes (though from the pricing structure of beer it had pretensions to be). From the very brief snapshot I had of Greece I concluded that the people were superb, but the country itself needed to pull its socks up and get organised. It was understandable, in a way, given their acute economic problems, but as I departed Thessaloniki, I hoped that whatever steps the country sought to take, they would work, as the people were terrific. I still had a fair bit of cycling to do in Greece but was now looking towards Turkey.

The trip across north Greece was uneventful, it took eight days to reach İstanbul. Aside from Kavala, which was an attractive coastal town, there was precious little to see. Much of the landscape was semi-arid and desert-like. The heat was intense with low 40's every day, which just came at you off the road surface. I was disappointed with Greece. The roadsides were covered with litter and fly tipping was evident everywhere. There appeared to be a general lack of pride. It looked neglected. Even in Turkey, guys were bagging litter especially near the towns. It was not all negative however, and the people were nothing but hospitable. Just outside Xanthi there was a Shell garage run by a husband and wife. The wife was an absolute delight and could speak English. We chatted about my trip and on saying goodbye she came out with two litres of peach juice and two litres of water and refused any payment. By the end of my tour through Greece I had been chased by dogs on nine occasions, the final one was through the centre of Alexandropoulos. Fortunately, it was early in the morning, but I knew it provided the locals with considerable entertainment and a smile over their coffee as I pedalled madly through the centre, big dog in hot pursuit, eyes fixed on my calf. As I cycled out of the country, I met the first cyclist doing what I was doing. Robbie from Scotland was also heading to İstanbul and he mentioned that he had had the same problem with dogs in Greece!

The border gantry proudly displayed a 'Welcome to Turkey' flag above it. It was always an adventure heading into a new country, discovering a different culture with new smells and sights. During the last 6km cycling on the A2 motorway to the Turkish border, only 12 cars passed me by. It was great having three lanes to myself and crossing the border was no problem, I just had to pay 15 euros for a visa at the gate. The signboard at the border announced that the distance to İstanbul was 236km. Much of the road was switchback with steep gradients of 1:7. For my first night I stayed in Keşan, where the first visible signs of urbanisation were blocks that looked almost soviet in style. My time coincided with Ramadan, but I still managed to find a cheap hotel where I ate and crashed out.

There was little incentive to explore the town, so I left the following day. It turned out to be one of the worst days of the entire tour. I got ready to set off for 8.15am, only to find that Cynthia had a flat rear tyre. I could not locate the puncture, so I decided it must have been the inner tube and changed it. After half an hour on the road, I had another puncture in the rear tyre! By 10.45am I was up and running, cursing over the wasted time. I had no option but to cycle the 77km to Tekirdağ, which was not the most attractive town. In decent conditions the distance could have been done in less than four hours, I had no such luck. The combination of switchback roads and a vicious gale force headwind meant that it took over ten hours to complete the day's run, and wow, did I know I had been on a ride. The conditions couldn't have been more different the following day, so I took the decision to get to İstanbul and cycled the remaining 147km in a respectable time. I was cycling on a reasonably busy local road, with 30km to go, when I came over the crest of a hill to see the city of İstanbul spread out before me. I was met with a cacophony of noise and vehicular chaos. The road immediately turned from a two-lane road into a one-way six-lane highway and I found myself in the middle of it. 'Forget the road rules, drive as hard as you can', seemed to be the local mantra. İstanbul did have a poor reputation for road safety. One driver really cut me up, so much so that I could almost feel the car touching and still he put the horn on me! About 300 yards ahead the lights turned red, so I managed to catch him and somewhat unbecoming of my nature, I smacked his door with my fist several times to draw his attention and gave him a mouthful of good old British verbal. He did not give me eye contact and shot off when the lights turned green. The bus driver alongside had clearly been watching the situation unfold. He shouted across what I guessed was the equivalent of "brilliant" and gave me the thumbs up.

As I looked towards the minarets in the distance, I have to say, I felt chuffed to have made it as far as I had. The final stretch into İstanbul was incredibly tough to cycle and it was touch and go as to whether I was bounced into the next lane on several occasions. Still, I made it in, and could finally relax for a few days, enjoy some beers and explore Europe's largest city (although some of it extended into Asia). I found my way to the Blue Mosque, which was an area popular with backpackers and tourists. Needless to say, there were numerous hostels and small hotels in the vicinity around Taksim Square. I was spoilt for choice and struck lucky with a gem overlooking the Bosporus. I was just about teetering on the edge of Europe and could see Asia across the water.

I found the drivers in Turkey to be very courteous, with the understandable exception of İstanbul of course although even those were generally okay. Everyone wanted to start a conversation with me; to get my attention they put the horn on me, not for me to get out the way but to say hello and wave or shout things like, "where are you from?". Motorcyclists too, often came alongside and tapped me on the shoulder with encouragement. Most thought I was German (so did the Greeks), so when I told them I was English they would say "Ah Rooney, Manchester!". My reply, of course, was "No, not Rooney or Manchester, it's Plymouth!", I was met with "Ah Plymut, yes Plymut". I hoped to have more conversions from the Turkish club Galatasaray to the Green Army!

The hostel was very comfortable and provided everything I needed. I did all my washing and overhauled Cynthia in an open basement area where she was securely kept. The staff were wonderful, always chatting and friendly. Once I had recovered and felt fresh, I began to consider the next move. Thoughts ran through my head; 'Was that an end to it? Do I head back now, or do I get the Asia map out and keep going?'. I felt very fit, I was enjoying the challenge, and the idea of crossing the Bosporus into a new Continent was very appealing. In the end, the decision wasn't that hard. I would keep going.

I wanted to cycle through Iran, but I knew that was likely to prove problematic given the political stance between Iran and the UK. I had heard so many good things about Iran and its people that I would have loved the opportunity to revisit the country. I was last there in the 1970s via the Magic Bus en route to India. The general consensus appeared to be that holding a UK or USA passport was not conducive to the most favourable approach from Iran. Of course, I could understand this given the politics, but from a very selfish and personal viewpoint, it was a great shame. I visited the Iranian consulate and was advised that I'd need a Ministry document (effectively a letter of introduction) before I could even think about a visa. This could be applied for online but would take between eight and ten working days, then I'd still have to go through the visa process. In total, the whole exercise could take three weeks with no guarantee as to the outcome. I thought, initially, that I might get lucky at the Consulates at either Trabzon or Erzurum, but it was a gamble. I got chatting to an Iranian who had a UK passport and wanted to visit family in Iran. He was still on his 5th day of waiting and told me they were messing him about because he was a UK passport holder. He was convinced I would get the same treatment. Looking at the map, an alternative route was to head for Georgia, Armenia, Azerbaijan and perhaps, if Iran was a no go, I could fly over to Kazakhstan or India.

For the bike enthusiasts reading this, I had counted four punctures in total by this point. They happened in Ancona, Alexandroupoli, two were in Keşan, plus I had one tyre ripped in the Czech Republic. Having decided to continue, I made a number of purchases to improve the ride on Cynthia. I replaced the Brooks saddle as the rivets had quite literally become a pain in my backside! One of the best extras I bought was an additional mirror. I also picked up a few spares and ditched 6kg of gear. This, I have to confess, was a bit drastic but given the climate and other factors I didn't think I would need it, so courtesy of TNT it went back to the UK. I was left with around 18-20kg which was pretty light for the trip. I felt sure that Cynthia would appreciate the gesture and hoped I wouldn't regret it.

My legs were particularly grateful for the respite in İstanbul, it was also a wonderful opportunity to wander around and explore an incredible city. The sights, sounds and smells were a heady mix of east and west, but it worked. Sitting around people-watching was always fascinating, it was especially so in İstanbul as it had so much to offer and was an international magnet for tourism. I was staying at the Orient Hostel, which along with many others sat behind the Blue Mosque. The view was excellent from the 3rd floor lounge area, and I only needed to turn 180 degrees to see the Bosporus. It was a convenient location and a great place to kick off the first couple beers of the day. I stuffed myself throughout the week. It was a great feeling being able to eat as much as I liked, knowing that any weight gained would be lost in a few days.

Staying at the hostel was an Irish feller called James. He was a great bloke who was a volunteer for UNICEF and was walking with a Maclaren kids' buggy (a Mothercare special) for UNICEF between Edinburgh and Dunedin (NZ). He had set off the previous January and had plans to stay in İstanbul for three weeks before hopefully reaching Dunedin two to three years later. Now that was a project! He was getting support from UNICEF along the way which was great. James had travelled a great deal, mostly roughing it along the way, so he was well equipped to succeed. He also intended to apply for an Iranian Visa but with an Irish passport it appeared that he would not have the same delays or hoops to jump through as I did.

I spread the map out on the table at the Orient Hostel for the last time, with a beer beside it, my route (and subsequent exclusion of Iran) was determined by default. The next day I planned to head for the Black Sea coast and cycle along its southern shore, whereupon I would cross into Georgia and Azerbaijan and head for Baku on the Caspian Sea. From there, unless I got hugely fortunate with visas for the Stans, it looked like I would have to fly to Almaty, or far more likely Delhi, and continue from there. But that was all for the future and no doubt fate would take a hand in the decision-making process. What I was sure of, was that the next day I was setting out for Asia!

In many ways, I was sad to leave the Orient Hostel as I had enjoyed staying there. I had made friends with several of the staff, two of whom gave me a small present the morning I left. They were such lovely people. I cycled leisurely down to the waterfront and purchased a ticket, boarding the ferry soon after. Halfway across the Bosporus I turned behind me and looked at the İstanbul I had just left and the Europe I was leaving behind. It felt like quite a leap with my journey heading into new territory. I turned back around and looked to where the ferry was pointing, to Asia and something completely different. Another challenge, another experience, this was what I had been looking for. Getting out of İstanbul proved as difficult as getting in. After several false starts, I linked up with the motorway and very quickly realised that to stay on that road was a death wish. It was very evident that the drivers were none too happy with my presence so at the first available opportunity I exited and linked up with the D100, which was the Old Road and ran parallel with the motorway. The D100 was no country lane either. It was a dual carriageway carrying a large volume of traffic, dust and muck, but from a cyclist's perspective it was more containable since there was at least a reasonable shoulder to ride on. I stayed with the D100 out of İstanbul (some 60km!) and kept with it for several hundred kilometres more before turning south to Çankırı at Ilgaz.

I continued to wild camp off the D100, which was fine, as there was nowhere else to stay. Now and then I'd come across a small town and try to find a hotel to shower and wash, but it wasn't always easy as I had veered well off the main tourist route. Most hotels charged between the equivalent of eight to fourteen pounds for a room with a shower and believe me, nothing beat the ability to enjoy a hot shower and rest up after a day on the road. There was also a breakfast, which generally consisted of bread and jam, sometimes it included cereal or the traditional Turkish breakfast of olives, cheese and meat. I would have died for the full English.

My map was basic, given to me at a Shell service station, it had no road definition whatsoever. It did give me the main road network to the larger towns and cities and sticking with the D100 proved to be the right decision, as I made my way towards the Caspian Sea and the city of Samsun (my advice to any cyclist crossing Turkey would be to stay with the D100). The road south of Ilgaz quickly turned into a single carriageway, which was preceded by an 8.7km hill climb. At the peak of the mountain, some 5,000ft plus, I was met by a thunderstorm, which continued for the best part of two hours and of course left me dripping wet. Yet within half an hour of the sun coming out, I was dry again. The repetition of cycling/walking over a mountain range became a regular feature right into Samsun. There was no point bothering about it, that was the way I had to go, so I just got on with it and enjoyed the scenery. That was the philosophy I adopted on each occasion with a few well-chosen expletives along the way. It was difficult terrain, and my progress was slow. The route between Çankırı and Çorum (about 150km) had to be done in two legs (and on two legs for much of it!). The first leg was grim, I cycled along the D180, which in title I assumed to be a major road, but it wasn't. The only people I saw were farmers and the very occasional melon seller. The landscape was almost lunar with bare rock and mountains, ridges, deep ravines, and formations of small saltpans. There was no habitation for miles, and I was effectively cycling over a plateau above 3,000ft. I knew some would admire the stark scape as beauty, but I was pleased to arrive in the mountain town of İskilip that evening.

Along the route and without exception I experienced, almost continuously, the usual vehicular (use of horn) and verbal chiacking, notably with passing trucks, workmen and well just about everyone. Pulling into a petrol station and parking by a pump always went down very well. The guys at the petrol station would serve chi. Little English would be spoken, but enough for the usual questions of "Where are you from?" or "Where are you going?". I was always treated with a degree of curiosity and the locals enjoyed taking a close look at Cynthia (despite her looking a little road worn and rough round the edges)! On two occasions I asked garage owners if I could sleep on their premises and neither had any problem with my request. The locals did not advocate wild camping and warned me to be selective where I fixed my tent, because wild dogs were prevalent throughout the area. I did see two packs on my route; one was chasing and attacking a herd of cattle, and the other pack of four noticed me cycling alongside. Fortunately, there was a high wall on the pass I was climbing and I was soon able to begin my descent at speed.

It was in this region where I got chased by two farm dogs. Having just reached the summit of a hill, I began to descend. Looking to my right I saw an isolated farm, almost half a kilometre away on the plain. I noted two tracks to the farm, one I was approaching and the second lay a few hundred yards towards the bottom of the hill. I heard barking and saw two dogs come out of the building. I quickly appraised my surroundings as I knew they had spotted me. There was nowhere to hide, my only thought was to cycle down the hill as fast as I could and hope to outrun them. With an adrenaline rush you would not believe, I hit the pedals with everything I had. My speedometer showed 93km/h down this very steep hill. The dogs sensed the chase and ran along the lower track to meet me as I passed. I kept going, knowing that if I was caught or fell off, I was in serious trouble. As I approached the junction with the track, the dogs were closing in fast. I kept pedalling for all I was worth. The dogs were about thirty yards behind me, so I got a good look at them. They were some sort of Rhodesian

Ridgeback, about the size of a wolf. They got to within about twenty yards and I could see their yellow teeth. I turned my attention to the road and didn't look anywhere but in front of me, making sure I didn't hit any potholes or slide off. I was now on level ground and my speed had slowed to about 56km/h. Thank goodness I was fit! I caught the dogs in my mirror, the gap having widened, but I kept going as hard as I could for the best part of another two kilometres until I felt sure I had left them behind. I am not religious, but I looked up to the heavens that day and said thanks. I felt exhausted but fortunate not to have been injured or worse.

Çorum was a major centre for the interior part of Turkey and held around 220,000 people. From there, the road improved all the way to Samsun. One thing that was noticeable was that Asian Turkey bore little resemblance to the European side of İstanbul, which had a significant European influence. The towns and villages gradually became more Middle Eastern in their way of life. The people also reflected this, although Samsun and Trabzon were more cosmopolitan. The news was all about the Middle East and looked eastwards rather than towards Europe. Religion also played a more important role in this society than I had imagined. It was highlighted during my tour because of Ramadan, which was soon coming to an end.

I met one or two real characters along the way. Radvan owned a cafe and ice cream parlour in Çankırı. I happened to pull in by his café to stop for a short break. Well, that was it, he virtually hauled me off Cynthia and into a chair. He got me a coffee and showed me his geology collection, which wasn't the first thing I would have guessed. Having studied geology, I was familiar with some of the crystalline structures and was able to discuss them with him. This almost sent him into a frenzy, and he shot back into the shop and pulled out two large books; one a photo album with Radvan and notaries and dignitaries and an autograph book which had all sorts of entries. There was only one entry in English, but that soon became two as he asked me to pen a sentence and sign. He enquired about my accommodation and when I asked for a suggestion, he shouted for his son in the shop who immediately got on his scooter and took me to what looked like the best hotel in town. He spoke to the receptionist and after smiling and saying goodbye, said not to worry, that I was a special guest, then he left me. I had no idea what the room rate for the hotel was, but I am certain I did not pay anything close to it.

While hauling Cynthia up a mountain I saw a scooter lying on its side on the opposite side of the road. Suddenly, the owner came out from behind a bush, smiling, waving and shouting. He called me over and with a mixture of hand movements and other gesticulations I found out that he had broken down and was waiting for a mechanic. He offered me a beer, which surprised me, since he was from Azerbaijan, I guessed that was why he was behind the tree enjoying a swift half! He had a whacking great sunflower head and showed me how to take the seeds from the flower by biting a certain way so that the husks came apart and you could spit them out, retaining the kernel. He also showed me which berries were good for marmalade and for easing aches and pains.

It was strange what my mind turned to whilst cycling, and the routine I got into. I always looked ahead to spot potholes or glass, which were common problems, then I would eye either side of the road in a sweep and take in the views from both in-front and behind (making use of Cynthia's mirrors). I followed this routine almost constantly.

It took me ten days to cycle from the Bosporus to Samsun. It wasn't the easiest ten days cycling. In fact, it was challenging. The geography, road conditions and prevailing wind conspired to give the impression that no matter how far İ cycled, İ always felt İ was going backwards, especially when I studied the map and saw how relatively little distance I had travelled at the end of each day. Over a three day period, I cycled 360km yet it appeared I had hardly made a dent on the map.

From crossing the Bosporus I had not seen a single cyclist, so when I passed by not one, but two cyclists on my way into Samsun, I stopped immediately! They introduced themselves as Claudia and Toby, they were from Germany and had been riding since June, following the Danube Trail before heading to the Ukraine and Russia, where they had then taken a ferry to Trabzon. They were on their way south and west to İstanbul before heading back to Germany. They were very helpful, giving me sound advice on what to expect between here and Trabzon. They also reckoned it was worth checking out the Iran Consul in Trabzon, since it appeared that they were more relaxed than İstanbul. I had to wait and see, but I hoped the Brits were a bit more flavour-of-the-month over there. Samsun itself was a vibrant city of 600,000 on the Black Sea. A three course meal cost five pounds. Portions were large, just what the doctor ordered.

I spent a very enjoyable rest day in Samsun, which was a bustling commercial city and port. I walked along the seafront and explored the central area. Historically Samsun had been frequented by the Hittites and apparently there were significant archaeological ruins yet to be uncovered from the area. Samsun was also known as the home of the Amazons, fearless female warriors who fought on horseback with arrows. It was said that these fearsome ladies would cut off a breast so that their aim would be true. Drastic in anyone's book I would say!

Cynthia and I left Samsun around 8.30am and, having negotiated the usual city traffic, we found ourselves cruising on a decent shoulder lane on a dual carriageway: the D010. Sometimes the elements conspired to give me every break possible and this day was one of those. I had warm sun on my back with frequent cloud cover, a tail wind and a level road. The Black Sea was never far from my left vision. I looked at my onboard computer and I was cruising with ease at around 20mph. It was the perfect way to cycle. Never taking the elements or topography for granted, I made sure to put in a good few kilometres before taking a break. I need not have worried, nothing changed during the day and I passed through many small coastal towns. While in Samsun I got chatting to the owner of a mini market who was an ex-seafarer, mainly based on the Aegean and around İzmir. He told me that the Black Sea was very polluted and not ideal to swim in, which explained the lack of people in the sea.

Towards the end of the day, just before reaching Ordu, I had a choice to make, to go through a new tunnel, which was some 3km long or take the old road around the coast and hinterland, which would provide a 19km detour. I was not a fan of tunnels. Toby and Claudia had come through that way and said it was fine, but they also had reflective jackets. Apparently, the sensors could pick up cyclists and automatically switch on more lights at each section (something I imagined could only be of German design) so Toby and Claudia felt fine about the experience. Well, the weather was good, and the map indicated there were a few coastal villages, so I went with the coast route. It was worth the detour, however, as with all routes that have been bypassed, the micro economy of the villages had really suffered. Most people were gathering and sorting hazelnuts, a key crop in the area. The consequence of taking the route almost certainly deprived me of attaining 200km for the day's ride. I cycled into Ordu having done 180km, which wasn't bad in any case. The road cut straight through the coastal city, which was home to about 150,000. As I pulled up to the lights in the city centre, dusk started to form. I hauled Cynthia up onto the pavement and parked her up by the Tourist Information Office. I managed to fix up accommodation very reasonably, with an en-suite sea view room for eight pounds sterling.

The day I arrived in Ordu was the final day of Ramadan. I had found, from my time living and working in the UAE, that the longer Ramadan progressed, the worse the driving became. It certainly seemed the case in Turkey and it may have been a coincidence, but I witnessed three accidents that day. The general standard of erratic driving made me decide to stop cycling at that point. I saw a Mondeo veer off to the right in a town centre and go straight into a ditch. There were loads of people around and the driver was fortunate no one was injured, luckily there was also a traffic police point literally 30 yards beyond the incident. The two other accidents were shunts involving several cars at lights. The Turkish drivers had this impulse to always be ahead, it wasn't quite as bad as the Italians but then in my opinion the Italians were better drivers. In the UK, if a car were to approach a right-hand junction it would usually pull up behind whatever was in front and turn off. In Turkey, the cars would career past then cut right across in front of me! I became familiar with the tactic, so always kept my eyes on Cynthia's mirror. I learnt that Turkish drivers would also open their car door without checking their mirrors. This was commonplace, and one car very nearly sideswiped me as I passed. When I turned around the driver was very apologetic. No harm had been done, so I continued on with a thumbs up.

As good as the day was cycling into Ordu, it was as bad the following day. By 10am the clouds had gathered with a vengeance and not long after they unleashed their furore on me. It chucked it down all day and without waterproofs I got soaked, mind you with them it wouldn't have made much difference. It was very noticeable that the second part of the journey (the 180km to Trabzon) contrasted greatly with the first leg in relation to the coastal towns. Between Ordu and Trabzon the road bypassed each town but was separated by a barrier. Without exception, all of the towns were falling into various states of neglect and disrepair. There was no incentive whatsoever for me to stop and look around. Rubbish piled up on open ground and buildings were in poor or unfinished condition.

For the last 100km or so to Trabzon there were no hotels, all had closed. I made my way through a series of five tunnels extending from 200m to 2.6km in length (for safety reasons I walked these) and then Cynthia got a puncture in her back wheel again. On closer inspection I noted two broken spokes as well. I walked on a bit until I saw a restaurant set back from the road. To the side of the restaurant was a partly covered lean to store which afforded some shelter from the deluge that was taking place. I started to strip her down. It wasn't an ideal place to remove the lady's covering but needs must, she was a rough old bird! I fixed the puncture ok, for the second time it was a strip of wire that had penetrated the tyre. I had purchased spokes from the bike shop in England but they were too long and were for the front tyre only. I should have checked before I left but what happened, happened. All I could do was ride Cynthia gently until we reached Trabzon. While I was carrying out the surgery, the restaurant owner's daughter came over. She was about twelve and called Zainab. She spoke perfect English and attended a school in İstanbul. Whilst fixing the bike, I cut my hand quite badly without realizing. Zainab noticed and went back to her house to return with a wipe and various plasters, which she insisted on applying herself. I asked her what she wanted to do when she finished school, she said "Be a doctor".

As I mentioned, there were no hotels for the final 100km or so into Trabzon. That was fine, if I'd had that information upfront but of course I didn't. Mindful of the impending darkness that was beginning to fall, I pulled off the main road and cycled through two or three villages to see if by chance any had accommodation for the night. At one of the villages, someone said, "Ah yes, the teaching house". It sounded great to me, I had stayed at a similar sort of University accommodation before and it had been fine. I received directions and started to make my way, asking again for instructions a couple streets later. Eventually I found the building and parked Cynthia. As I dismounted, I was met by the two people I had originally asked for directions plus at least three others. They all accompanied me inside where I met the manageress and asked if she had a bed for the night.

"No", came the polite rebuttal.

"No?" I repeated!

"No, it's a student dorm, so no outsiders".

"Ah, well then what are my options?" I asked.

At this point everyone had joined in the discussion, in Turkish of course. My arrival seemed to cause a bit of interest for some reason. Five more people walked in (which made ten in total). Luckily one could speak fluent English, his name was Yusef and he was accompanied by members of his family who were delightful. He explained the position to me, then told me to wait. At this point I spoke up, directing my words to the manageress.

"I don't want to cause you any problems, I saw a couple of tents on the beach, I'm very happy to head over there for the night."

In unison the reply from everyone was, "No, no, no, dangerous, you will be attacked."

Following some negotiation, the taking of my passport details and assurances from myself as to the reason why I was cycling (which they loved), the manageress let me have a whole four-bed dorm to myself for seven lira (about two pounds). Yusef also insisted on giving me his phone number, saying that if I had any problems in Turkey to call him and that if I returned to İstanbul, I could stay at his family flat. He also came with me to the shops to make sure I wouldn't get ripped off. How could I begin to thank people who were so kind? They really put themselves out on a limb for me and I was so grateful.

The ride into Trabzon the following morning was a breeze and the bad weather from the day before had cleared up. I rode at a sedate pace and was careful, knowing that Cynthia had two rear spokes missing. I found my bearings and checked in to a hostel in the city centre. Trabzon was one of Turkey's major regional centres, and had over one and a half million residents. I planned to stay a few days, which may have felt excessive if not for the fact that the first two days were residue from the public holiday for Ramadan. It meant that I couldn't visit the Iran Consul until the day after. Whilst waiting I bumped into two English speaking Turkish students, who took it upon themselves to help me find a bike repair shop. Once again, I found the kindness of strangers extraordinary. The shop fixed the bike and gave Cynthia an overhaul in the main square, which aroused some interest from the locals wandering past.

I finally made my way to the Iran Consulate, buoyed with a little more optimism after having spoken with Toby and Claudia. I reckon the whole episode at the Consulate took the best part of 47 seconds! Following the traditional good morning greetings, the official asked me where I was from.

"England", I replied.

"No visa," he responded, "not for UK or USA".

So that was a firm no! The consular official, who was perfectly polite, advised me that even if I had got a letter of introduction, I would never have been granted a visa. The three Swiss people filling in their applications looked up and were clearly surprised at the immediate refusal. So, there I had it, my path was set for Georgia and Azerbaijan. For my final two days in the city I continued to consume huge quantities of McDonalds chocolate milkshakes, which did just the job to improve the calorie intake. I'd been dreaming about them since İstanbul.

About a week after leaving Trabzon, I arrived in the Georgian capital of Tbilisi. Whilst crossing the border at Sarpi I immediately noticed the contrast between the two countries. I had become used to the semi-arid conditions in Turkey, and whilst cycling into verdant green territory I noticed familiar species including ferns, lilac and avenues of horse chestnut which were turning to their autumn plumage. The main road was a single carriageway and the vegetation encroached onto the road making me feel far more part of the landscape. Nineteen kilometres in, I came to the main border city of Batumi which lay on the Black Sea coast. It was undergoing development, although had retained much of its former character with markets and street traders jostling against one another along potholed roads. The area appeared chaotic with taxis and minibuses fighting for space and passengers. The whole scene was further complicated by the traders themselves pushing carts of various size and description, carrying an array of produce. Batumi had a familiar border town feel and I sensed the proliferation of hotels was directed more to visitors from over the border enjoying the nocturnal entertainment.

In Turkey I had found the locals very forthcoming in their salutations. In Georgia they were much more reserved and tended to watch you as you went by. The horns still sounded but I quickly realised that the majority were either wanting me out of the way or beeping to let vehicles ahead of them pass. The driving, which was unbelievably bad, was accentuated by a single carriageway that ran 15km west of Gori and beyond to Tbilisi for another 90km. The Turks knew how to build good roads, but in Georgia there was virtually no shoulder to ride on. If I was lucky, I managed about a foot in places and all the while I was negotiating potholes and tarmac ridges which could throw me all over the place. As for the driving itself, one thing I did note was how few women I saw behind the wheel. The only rule of the road was that there were no rules! Drivers seemed to have one gear (very fast) and one aim and that was to get in front of the vehicle ahead, whatever the cost. Drivers would steam right up to the vehicle in front and announce their presence with a horn. It was not uncommon for three vehicles alongside each other to come towards me whilst two or three in a line came up behind me at the same time, surrounding me from all sides. It was like a game of chicken and must have been a macho thing, but it did keep me on my toes that's for sure. The situation was further compounded by free ranging cows and pigs that grazed along the roadside and often wandered across as they fed. You would have thought it would cause carnage, but it didn't. The only road casualties were dogs, whose bodies littered the road. If I had hired a car, it would have taken me some time to adjust to the Georgian school of motoring, but I had the feeling Georgians knew how to react, it was mayhem, but it worked. However, they had no regard whatsoever for cyclists, they chopped me up, cut across me and stopped right in front of me as if I wasn't there. The strange thing was that when I finally made it to the dual carriageway, there was suddenly adequate road space. The horns stopped, and the driving seemed much more controlled.

After leaving Batumi I cycled along the coast towards Poti. It was almost, but not quite like riding in England and unlike Turkey the villages fronted right onto the road. The melon vendors gradually morphed in to pottery vendors. Poti itself was nothing to write home about, it was a sprawling old style city, again with the focus on the market street scene. On my ride in, I was struck down by my third puncture in almost as many days. "Cynth", I said, "this cannot go on". Two fellers came over and since it was clear what was needed, they insisted on taking me to the bike shop. I followed them through dirt streets, either side of which were crowded tin, stone and concrete framed shops selling all sorts, with displays on the road itself. Just about every square inch was used. Hens clucking and pigs squealing added to the contained chaos. As it was early morning, the womenfolk were out looking for the best produce on offer. I purchased a new tyre, not a top quality one by any means, but as I intended to fit the 2.25" tyres, either in Tbilisi or Baku, I hoped that Cynthia would last the few hundred kilometres until then.

My route followed the main road, it was the only road between Poti to Tbilisi. Despite the traffic, I made good mileage. One night I pulled into a small town and found a hotel. It didn't look like much, but it provided a bed and a shower. Breakfast was the traditional sausages although shortly after leaving I developed serious stomach cramps and had to dive behind the nearest vegetation. Whatever it was just went straight through me and was a distinctive bright yellow! I felt decidedly off colour for the rest of the day, and consequently cycled nowhere near my daily average. The following evening I was still miles from any town or village, so I began searching for suitable off-road accommodation and somewhere to camp. Ahead, on my right, there were drainage works in progress, although there was no sign of human activity on site. Set back from the road were two large concrete pipe sections so I pulled over to take a closer look. It seemed absolutely perfect. The pipes were big enough for me to wheel Cynthia in under cover and set out my sleeping bag, there was plenty of space and it was dry. It was a five star drain and couldn't have been better. Hidden from view, with the rain pouring down, I settled in the knowledge that I had made the right decision to stop cycling earlier than planned. It was well before nightfall but I was dry. The position of the pipe meant there was limited chance of any rain pouring in, so I tucked myself up in the sleeping bag ready to enjoy a comfortable and undisturbed night's sleep. In the morning, feeling much refreshed, I cycled into Kutaisi for some food, my stomach grumbling all the way. I was hungry since I hadn't eaten in over 24 hours since the previous breakfast (and that hadn't stayed in very long)!

Kutaisi was a large city that had undergone a modern resurgence. More importantly it had a McDonalds, not that that proved anything but at that particular time it was manna from above. Just as I arrived for breakfast the heavens opened with a belter of a storm that continued unabated all day. The streets quickly flooded and as the cars drove by, they completely showered the pedestrians from head to foot without a thought! I was in a bit of a dilemma, having to decide if I should I stay and consume more and more chocolate shakes and coffee or go for it. I went for it and cycled the distance I needed to get to Zestafoni. It was unfortunate that I was told there was a hotel further in Kharagauli, some 25km distant. Well, there wasn't! The town, which was situated in a steep valley, miles away from the main road, ended in a dirt track and the police politely advised me to go back to where I'd come from. So, I did.

The time wasted meant that I was wild camping again, although fortunately, set back in trees I noticed a somewhat dilapidated timber structure resembling a shack (but it was quaint in its homespun way, the dry rot and damp added to the experience)! I did not need much encouragement to get up at 5am the next day and began heading towards Gori. Along the way I saw a signboard with distances in kilometres to Tbilisi, Yerevan and Tehran. What might have been!

The road to Gori was mountainous. There was a cool breeze as I started my ascent up to 1,400m, encouraging Cynthia to get her finger out. A van pulled up beside us and offered a lift into the next town of Khashuri some 20km ahead. I took up the kind offer, reckoning that I was owed a few kilometres from the previous day. I also thought it would be good to gain a driver's perspective, even if that meant looking through a very cracked windscreen! The ride went as expected, my driver wanted to drive as fast as he could and overtook on sharp bends (since surely nothing would be coming the other way), he went down a 1:7 and didn't consider braking, finding it more prudent to accelerate instead. But we got to Khashuri in one piece and the drive saved me a day of cycling, so I was very grateful.

The city of Gori had considerable character despite most of its buildings dating from the immediate post war period. Inevitably, during my sojourn across Georgia it became clear that my favourite Russian architect had again been unleashed in designing some really ugly industrial plants and high-rise tenements clad in concrete and tin! How the Soviets put satellites into space, I will never know. Gori most notably was the birthplace of Stalin and the city did not appear to have changed much from his era.

The ride from Gori into Tbilisi was great, the road was decent, I enjoyed ideal weather and Cynthia and I knocked off the eighty kilometres in under three and a half hours averaging around 23km/h (which was pretty good going). It was easy to find the city centre, although it was effectively divided by the river. Some of the architecture was beautiful, especially the Government and Public Buildings; there was a good feel to the city. As you would expect in a capital city, all the major players were present including the big hotel chains. Getting across the arterial roads was difficult, as cars would not stop for you to cross. I planned to stay for a while, this was in part enforced by my need to obtain an Azerbaijan Visa, but I also wanted to meet my ex-boss Steve, who was flying in from Kazakhstan the week after. I looked forward to catching up with him again. I had been advised that visas for Azerbaijan had been difficult to get for some reason. I hoped it wouldn't be a problem. My back up was to bus it to Yerevan and pick up an Indian Visa, although if I had an Armenian stamp the Azerbaijanis wouldn't let me in! Armenia (Christian) and Azerbaijan (Muslim) were not good mates. After arriving in Tbilisi, I tallied up my total distance and found out I'd cycled 6,087km. It was a statistic to be proud of.

I found a hostel in the old part of the city. Prices were much more expensive than in Turkey. The woman at the hostel (Waltzing Matilda) was as rude as you could possibly get, she was completely offhand and couldn't have cared less, refusing to let me bring Cynthia into the building. Since it was late, I decided to stay the night but after depositing my stuff in the room, I went out to look for alternative accommodation and wandered into the Liberty Hostel nearby. I was able to book a four-bed dorm to myself with a balcony from the next day. Since I was older than most of the travellers they'd seen, they thought I would appreciate the extra room for the same money. They had no issue with Cynthia, and I was shown where I could safely leave her inside the hostel under lock and key.

The following morning, I checked out of the Waltzing Matilda and bumped into the owner, Tatiana, who was delightful, so I explained why I was leaving. In the Liberty I met an Aussie called Justin. He was a top bloke who had only arrived the night before. He had been travelling for fourteen months and had some great experiences and a lot of information helpful to my onward progress.

I remained in Tbilisi for three weeks and managed to meet up with Steve, who was over to spread his empire and open another office under the Veritas Brown/Cushman & Wakefield banner. He was keen to have me assist, though in what capacity I wasn't sure. In the meantime, I made the most of the late summer weather and explored the city.

My hostel was situated just off Rustaveli Avenue, a mainly tree lined avenue which formed the main road through the city centre. The architecture along the avenue was generally striking, very attractive and European in feel and design. There was a lot of building activity taking place in and around the city. It appeared to be on the back of considerable international investment in recent years, mainly from Washington. Georgia really did appear to be open for business. No visas were required for many nationalities and apparently it was the third easiest place in the world to start a business (New Zealand ranked top), which was surprising given that it was ex-Soviet Union (ID papers and stamps were needed in volumes across many of the former states). There were a lot of Americans in the city, although the bulk of tourists appeared to be mainly Israeli and Polish.

The city offered the usual high street brands that were familiar in the UK, including Next, Mothercare and Bata, as well as small independents. Beneath the Canadian Consulate, set back from Rustaveli Avenue, stood Prospero's, the best patisserie/coffee shop and bookstore in the city. It soon became my morning pilgrimage and doubled up as a great meeting place. I enjoyed several conversations with Americans over coffee. One in particular was a young lady called Camilla, she had recently qualified as an architect from DC and was typically enthusiastic! She was a real delight! As well as increasing my caffeine intake I did some research into my next route, which ended up being a process of elimination. Geographically, I had hit something of an impasse since I was unable to proceed through Iran. It was a great shame, not simply because of the convenience and directness of route, but because I had heard nothing but positive and glowing tributes as to how beautiful the country was and how friendly and welcoming the people were. I met several Iranians in Tbilisi, one couple were staying at my hostel, and they were charming, ready to extend a cordial invitation to stay with them if I ever got the chance to enter their country. The other factor, apart from geography, was cost. I didn't have the luxury of too much time or bottomless pockets, so this also became a consideration.

I looked into heading through the 'stans, cycling up to Almaty then flying to Delhi, since by the time I would hit Almaty the winter would have kicked in, making crossing the Himalayas unlikely. The cost to get into Azerbaijan was US$174, that was where I needed to go to collect the various 'stans visas and I estimated that the additional cost would be in excess of US$500. Plus, I would need an air flight and had to factor in living expenses. The other practical problem was that it was likely I would only get a five day visa for Turkmenistan. It would be necessary for me to cycle across 476km of desert in that time, to the Uzbek border, and I wasn't overly confident that my geriatric legs could do the job. I knew it could be done but wasn't confident that I could. So, my conclusion was to leave Tbilisi and fly to Dubai to stay for a week where I could hopefully obtain an Indian Visa. From there I would fly on to Delhi. From Delhi I would start pedalling hard and cycle to Kolkata, along the north route into the tea plantation areas. I also wanted to visit places like Varanasi. From there I planned to head into Southeast Asia where I could then gauge first-hand how best to access the countries. Bangkok was the principal hub to collect a number of visas, but none were difficult to obtain. Myanmar, Laos, Cambodia, Vietnam and China were all on my list. I then had a choice of whether to continue to China, South Korea or Japan, or take a right and drop into Australia. That decision could wait though. And so, I decided on my game plan in outline. By heading straight to India I was in effect, only missing out on Iran and Pakistan. It was a big chunk on the map, but, in my defence, I had visited both countries before.

One day I will grow into this! Tbilisi, Georgia

9

THE EARLY DAYS

Coming Home

My career with the Merchant Navy came to an end at the ripe old age of twenty-six. As I looked out of the window, on the train back to Ilfracombe, my mind turned towards the future. I was beginning to think that I needed to consider a more permanent career move. I still had no qualifications and no idea what to do with my life. To rectify this state of affairs, I stayed with a favourite Aunt while working and studying for GCE's. Following which, I moved to Plymouth and studied for A levels at Devonport CFE.

The age difference was never a barrier at college. I greatly enjoyed studying with the other students, who were some ten years younger than myself. I became good friends with several of them, who to this day keep in contact. I had rented a room in Keyham which was on the way to the college and two of my classmates, Si and Dave, would call in regularly. Revision time was always an event. Their arrival around 10am coincided with coffee plus three glasses and a large bottle of scotch. I am not sure how but it worked, as we all somehow passed and attained the grades we needed. A lot of the guys at college were also keen to play rugby. Being a CFE, there were no organised teams, so Si, Dave, Charlie Cobbold and I set about establishing one. We had no problem finding fifteen players of various shapes and sizes, the difficulty was finding any opposition to play us. After some persuasion, I managed to arrange a match with Plymstock School 1st's. Our team turned up in an array of different shirts. We were consequently named 'the multi-coloured swap shop' by the opposition (after a Saturday morning TV show). We got stuffed 64-3, so there ended our sporting ambitions. Charlie took the defeat to heart and subsequently emigrated to Australia to be a sheep farmer.

After college, I was accepted to read Geology at Manchester University. It soon became apparent that any career opportunity would be somewhat restricted to core logging in the North Sea and given my age (29), I decided to transfer to Portsmouth Polytechnic to study for a cognate degree in surveying. Surveying appealed as, like Geology, it was an outdoor career. However, the scope of work was still diverse enough for me to find, and specialise in, a field of interest. I obtained a degree in 1983 and at the age of thirty-three set out on a career path.

I began serving a three year apprenticeship with Devon County Council in Exeter. The job provided an excellent grounding in all aspects of the profession. Much of the work involved the management of Exeter Airport, which, given my proclivities for overseas travel was perhaps not ideal. However, by this time I had married in what was a whirlwind romance. I met Vanessa during my transfer from Manchester University to Portsmouth Polytechnic. She had recently moved from Northampton to her parents' place near Woolacombe and, like me, we ended up working at the Lee Bay Hotel near Ilfracombe for the summer. Three months later, on Christmas Eve 1980, we married. The reception was held in a 16th century cottage, it was all very romantic. We purchased our first house in Exmouth in 1983, while we were both working in Exeter. Then in 1986 our son Nick was born. The birth of our son coincided with the end of my articles and the attainment of my RICS status. I could easily have stayed on at Devon County Council, and I did think about it seriously. While it would have provided an almost job for life opportunity, something not to be taken lightly with a young family, I could not see a sufficient work challenge that would provide what I was looking for. I was keen to apply my knowledge to the hospitality sector, if I could, as I understood that industry well and had previous experience in it.

I decided to specialise in business appraisal work, a relatively new area of expertise in the profession. In addition to valuing land and property, I was required to have a clear understanding about how various businesses operated, incorporating the analysis of profit and loss accounts and balance sheets. I applied to Christie & Co in Exeter who were looking for valuers. I had hoped to stay in Exeter, for obvious reasons, however I was offered a managerial position for a new valuation department in Manchester and Leeds. Neither Vanessa nor I wanted to leave the West Country, but the opportunity was a challenge and appeared to be a good career move. We eventually moved to Lymm in Cheshire and I commuted via the M56 into Manchester. It provided a steep learning curve. I worked long hours networking and establishing the valuation department. In the end, our time in Manchester was determined by our son. His health had not been good since we moved north. He suffered from nasty and frequent chest infections. Coincidentally, a young couple we were friendly with, who also lived on the same road, were having a similar experience with their baby daughter. Our Doctor quietly admitted that the infections were most likely due to the clouds of chemicals being released in the air. They came over on the prevailing wind from Runcorn, a major centre for the chemical industry. Vanessa and I made the decision to leave and as good fortune would have it a good friend of mine in Plymouth had started working for a recently formed partnership called Tretheweys, which also specialised in business appraisal work. I approached the senior partner and was appointed a role based in Plymouth.

We had lived in Manchester for just over a year but were happy to be heading back to the South West once again. Our friends also moved quickly back to their former home in Oswestry. Within a few months there was no evidence of chest infections. It looked like the Doctor's diagnosis was spot on.

The following three years at Tretheweys were undoubtably some of the happiest in my professional working life. As the product developed and became more detailed, so the clients demanded more. I was working in a highly specialised and interesting sector of the profession. It was much more high risk and included valuing hotels, golf courses, nursing homes, retail premises and public houses. Inevitably, as a valuers' individual knowledge of different sectors increased, there was a natural progression to focus on, and develop individual specialisms. Over the years, my specialist areas concentrated on hotels, waterfront regeneration and marinas. In later years, in East Anglia, almost by default I became heavily involved with the equestrian sector. Unfortunately, the senior partners at Tretheweys overstretched themselves and the firm floundered with many redundancies and subsequent litigation with our clients, the banks.

Despite concerted efforts to settle and develop a career path, I could never shake off the desire to travel. It had always bubbled away and was never too far from the surface. I suppose the main problem was that I never really found that elusive career fit. I was always looking, but I never found that green light. How I envied (in a positive way) those who knew from day one where their destiny lay and were happy in their skin. I had always viewed my career as a means of making ends meet and meeting my responsibilities. I focused on enjoying what I did rather than doing what was needed to climb the greasy corporate pole. Despite the enjoyment, especially in the early years, my chosen career never provided the spark that I was looking for.

I have never deliberately embraced what some might call an unconventional lifestyle. Yet, when I have been presented with a conventional path, either fate or my decision making turned me against it. I have had accusations levelled towards me, by certain members of my family, that I have no discipline to settle to anything. Knowing the individuals concerned, I sensed a lot of innate jealousy as they looked inwards to their own lives and situation. In any event, achieving an MSc and FRICS in later life, frankly, dispelled that argument. No, I had not found that elusive career fit, but it did not stop me looking.

It was for this reason I sought a new opportunity in Canada in 1991. Having cold-called various property-based companies in Toronto, I managed to land a contract with an international real estate company called Drivers Jonas. They were keen to expand into the leisure sector and I found myself at the forefront carrying out hotel and leisure property valuations in Canada and the USA, including the

Grand Hyatt in San Francisco and the Sheraton in Toronto. My enthusiasm was short-lived as my wife had a change of heart and decided she did not want to leave England. As my son was only four years old at the time, staying in Canada would have meant I'd miss seeing him grow up so I reluctantly returned to England. I took various career breaks, including retraining as a secondary teacher during the mid-1990s. I subsequently studied for a Master's degree in Applied Marine Science. It increased my knowledge and specialism in waterfront regeneration, and I was able to apply it to my professional valuation and appraisal work. I enjoyed teaching, however family circumstances dictated that for financial reasons I had to give up after three years and return to surveying.

Looking back, living and working in Canada proved the catalyst for the breakdown in our marriage. Vanessa and I had grown apart, and returning on a permanent basis highlighted the gap that had been evident for some time during our relationship. I took my full share of responsibility for it, but knew it took two to tango. I walked and left Vanessa with the house as it was Nick's home. I had what I wanted which was unrestricted access to my son.

Trying to balance a career and parental responsibilities was difficult, especially when large distances were involved. Once Vanessa and I had formally separated, my work took me to Milton Keynes while she remained in the family home in Plymouth. My company, appreciative of the circumstances, allowed me considerable flexibility with my workload. So long as I hit the target for each month and the quality of work didn't suffer, they were happy for me to set off to Devon on Friday afternoons at around 2pm. I knew the MD well from our days working together at Tretheweys and, luckily, he was supportive of the situation. I would collect Nick and we'd arrive back at Milton Keynes by late evening. We always stopped for a Big Mac, double fries and a chocolate thick shake at Cribbs Causeway near Bristol. We spent many a Saturday evening during the winter months watching the Milton Keynes Kings Ice Hockey team (as they were then called) and football.

There was a period when I realised Nick was unhappy which, apart from our conversations, manifested itself around Sunday lunchtimes when we were about to set off to Devon and he became upset. I had wind of certain issues, concerning Vanessa's boyfriend, from a close neighbour who kept in contact with me, as her son and Nick were best mates. It reached a stage where it could not continue, so, unannounced, and having left Nick with the neighbour, I walked into our house and had what might be described as 'a frank exchange of views' with the individual concerned.

The summer holidays were wonderful, every year Nick and I camped for a fortnight at a superb site near Weybourne in Norfolk, it was always his choice. The park had everything, a heated pool, cycling tracks, vast expanses of heathland to roam and play and of course beaches nearby and fish and chip shops on Cromer Pier! We would play football after supper and as invariably happens, kids would meander over. We'd ask if they'd want a game and on they'd come. Gradually the pitch would fill up with girls and boys of all ages, in what often turned out to be a fourteen aside game. I used to ref, well, that is a loose translation, but I had the whistle. It became very popular, not just with the kids but also the parents who were able to crack open another bottle in peace before eventually hauling their offspring off the pitch to bed. In the mornings while I was in the ablution block, kids would enquire, "Is the game on tonight?". The answer was always "Yes!"

My son eventually came to live with me for several years which, from a personal point of view was a wonderful few years as we were (and still are) very close. Seeing him progress through secondary school, attain his GCSE's and A Levels was immensely satisfying. We enjoyed a very relaxed relationship, I cannot remember us ever arguing. His friends always enjoyed coming over for supper, especially if I was concocting a homemade pizza special. It usually incorporated melted marshmallow and chocolate and was liberally sprinkled with 'hundreds and thousands' with tons of Ben and Jerries to follow. To celebrate Nick's fifteenth birthday, we flew to Toronto, which he loved. We skated on frozen lakes and along the Rideau Canal in Ottawa in a balmy -15 degrees. I managed to reserve tickets for the Toronto Maple Leafs v Pittsburgh Penguins hockey game which was a complete surprise for him. His favourite team was the Pens. The following year we visited the west side of Canada to Banff, Calgary and Jasper. We found the best diners and ate stacks of delicious pancakes every morning, while we planned how we would spend the days. One February, we visited New York to be met with the third heaviest 24-hour snowfall the city had ever experienced. Before our eyes, parked cars along Broadway and 5th Avenue were completely covered as cross-country skiers took their place.

Back home, it always made me smile during exam revision times when I walked through the door to find several of Nick's 6th form friends draped around the lounge. They were all very friendly and often stayed for supper. Thank goodness for pizza and ice cream!

Nick and I knackered after a hard day on the beach

Nick and I catching supper

10

AND SO WE MOVE ON

India

I had made up my mind to head for India and planned to stop off in Dubai to pick up the appropriate visa. I left Tbilisi and headed for the airport. I had a flight booked with Qatar Airways who went out of their way to assist with Cynthia. I checked in early and a representative was only too happy to take all my gear and weigh it, indicating that it should be ok. Unfortunately, two panniers were not weighed, so when I checked in, I was considerably over the limit. Cynthia weighed in at 18kg which didn't leave much for me! After a very brief discussion they waived me through, no penalty was incurred as the flight wasn't full. I think seeing the charity tee shirt I was wearing may have held sway. It's always a real plus when airlines adopt a common sense and helpful stance.

I stopped off in Dubai for a week, staying with my ex-boss

Jonathan, his wife Carol and their three children who were lovely. I could not thank them enough for their hospitality, life was tough enough with a young family, so their kindness was so much appreciated. It had been over three years since I was last in Dubai and Abu Dhabi. Although by Middle Eastern and UAE standards growth had been modest following the economic crash, there were definite 'green shoots'. Projects were progressing. The metro in Dubai was open; buildings in progress were being 'topped off'; the Palm continued to be developed; there were several hotels under construction; while in Abu Dhabi, Reem Island was undergoing rapid transformation with the construction of the Gate; the new road from Yas Island to the airport was open and major residential developments had also progressed. So, it wasn't all doom and gloom, and while things were still relatively quiet for that part of the world, there was sufficient evidence to suggest that investors would still see the country as a place to do business.

My visa came through easily and so, with it in hand, I set off for the next adventure. It had been almost forty years since I last set foot in India. The visit had been a culmination of a two-year travel fest, where I had hitch hiked from Durban through Africa, to Greece, then across Turkey, to Iran (you could get in then with no difficulty, how times changed), Afghanistan, Pakistan via the Khyber Pass, and then India. By the time I arrived in India I was feeling run down. I travelled around Jammu and Kashmir visiting Srinigar and Lake Dal, but quickly ran out of steam. I caught pretty much every ailment India had to offer, to the extent that I did not feel well enough to visit any of the other amazing places the country laid claim to. I returned full of beans and ready to do battle with the road conditions, I couldn't wait to arrive in Delhi and kick start the journey again. There were many places I wanted to visit, so I didn't set myself a time limit, wanting to just savour the country. While I had enjoyed every aspect of the bike ride up till that point, I was looking forward to what lay ahead. To continue through Asia was a real prospect, I felt like a kid in a sweet shop not knowing which way to turn.

After being in Delhi for almost a week, I drew some initial conclusions about the country. From an objective point of view, I couldn't deny that India was the dirtiest country I had ever visited. Rubbish piles pervaded every street, except for the leafy areas where the Embassies were situated. Just about everywhere in towns and villages it was a common sight to see cows, pigs and dogs scavenging for something to eat on the rubbish piles. Yes, even the cows took to chewing cardboard boxes! The place smelled like a urinal. The reason became apparent when walking along Chelmsford Road, which linked New Delhi Station with Connaught Place. It was a common sight to see local fellers splashing their boots and other business along the wall and pavement, despite a free convenience being available a few yards away. Connaught Place was a circular central feature incorporating colonnades. In its day it would have been very imposing. While there were many international brands located within its walls, they were interspersed with local shops which were, invariably, run down and unattractive. In fairness, it didn't help that many of the roads were in various states of repair largely due to work on the metro. In the station and along many streets it was commonplace to see men and women crashed out on the pavement or set back on a softer dust pile. This unfortunately reflected the real India. India was considered an emerging economy with a growing population of 1.2 billion. I was sure it was true, but I had my doubts that a relatively small percentage of earners could continue making money at a pace where the fortunes of the burgeoning poor could be improved. This, to my mind, was the huge challenge India faced from the outset. Where I was staying and the way I was travelling meant that I got to see the real India, not the Bollywood that is sometimes portrayed. India remained a poor country, with a huge gulf between the few rich and the many poor.

Wandering around Delhi, I was immediately targeted as a tourist and therefore every tout made a beeline for me. I had no problem with the rickshaw cycles or the tuk-tuk drivers, who pulled up and invited me on board. Most were fine with a polite no thanks and a smile. With those that became more persistent I was firmer in response, but that was ok. The worst were the touts who sidled up alongside and started what they thought was a polite conversation, but

I knew it was the onset of a grilling; "Where are you from?", "Where are you going?", "What do you want to buy?".

88 Jaynath (off Connaught Place) was the only tourist bureau I trusted. I asked for a reputable place to book a tour and they recommended a Government agency in the Coffee Home two streets to the left of Jaynath. I booked the Agra tour on their recommendation. For fun I also tried one of the tout's recommendations, for comparative purposes, they wanted to charge me 8,500 rupees when the official operator charged 1,134 rupees and had included a guide. Entrance fees were on top, but they would have been in either case. The problem was that I became wary that everyone was a tout, the genuine people (of which I am sure there were many) became tarred with the same brush. There were signs everywhere not to deal with touts. It didn't exactly endear one to remain long in the place.

I took two tours, one to Jaipur and the other to Agra. I visited Jaipur by train which took about four hours and was cheap. The railway was the preferred local carrier, they said that some 500,000 people a day passed through Delhi station. The place was heaving, and the seventeen or so platforms all had trains with about the same number of carriages. It was necessary to book days in advance as every train was always full. Indian Railways was believed to be the world's largest employer with 1.4 million employees!

Jaipur itself was located some 250km to the west of Delhi in Rajasthan. I grabbed a taxi and did the sights including the Pink City, the Amber Fort and the Floating Palace. The latter two were some 16km from the city. I caught the sleeper train back to Delhi arriving at 5am. It was an experience and clearly well overbooked as the bunk I had booked was taken. This caused a point of discussion with other passengers, one of whom proceeded to unceremoniously poke the bag of rags on my bunk and drag it off. The bag of rags turned out to be an old lady. I immediately told the feller to stop, and said she was welcome to have the bunk. "No, she sleep on floor" he replied, to general consensus. "No, end of!" I replied and walked away. I got chatting to two Indian ladies and sat with them on their bunk until the conductor came along and asked me to regain my bunk or sit in its proximity. He then announced that the bunk the two ladies had booked was his and proceeded to invite the ladies to sleep on the carriage floor, which they did. Who said the age of chivalry was dead! An Indian lawyer who I subsequently met on the Agra tour mentioned that woman bashing was quite the thing in many households. The train stank of urine, the outside carriage doors were open, and men just peed into the wind or spat which was also a favourite activity.

Agra was an excellent trip, there were ten of us squashed into two microbuses. The journey there took about three hours with a breakfast stop and a chance to stroke a Cobra! We stopped off first at the temple at Sandhara, before arriving at the Taj Mahal. Agra itself was an unattractive city, as everywhere the cacophony of noise from traffic congestion was almost off the scale. The Taj seemed almost incongruous in its setting, although from the other side of the river it was spectacular. I loved the Arabic architecture, and the way the light broke through the building was breath-taking. It reminded me of the recently constructed Great Mosque in Abu Dhabi, a simply stunning building. Once through the queues and turnstile I was able to wander around in my own time and the Taj soon became one of my favourite places (along with Machu Picchu). The Red Fort was the final stop of the tour and was also hugely impressive, well, apart from an obligatory hustle into a marble shop. On the tour I met a young Chinese guy who was visiting India to purchase silver and other products to ship back to Shanghai. He kindly gave me his card with an invitation to call should I pass through. The journey back had its high spot too, since our vehicle was emitting blue smoke to the point where you couldn't see out the window. At the halfway point the smoke was making inroads into the vehicle itself, although the driver didn't seem to worry. We also had a shunt. The driver got out and chatted to the bloke who ran into us. He decided that the existing dents hadn't got any bigger, so they left it at that and drove off. Well, this was India!

The way I felt about things had nevertheless preyed on my mind since I arrived, and I started to drag my heels. In short, I bottled out of India. As with last time, I could not convince myself that I felt comfortable in its surroundings, and the more I thought about it, the more I really didn't fancy cycling across it. I subsequently booked a flight to Thailand and decided to head on from there. Yes, I felt like I was cheating, but I had no further desire to stay. They say India is mystical and has an abundance of interest and character. I tried my best to like the country, but I could not get away from what I perceived as its disadvantages. I still have regrets concerning my feelings for India. It is strange, I genuinely wanted to like the country and embrace everything it offered. I felt I had failed. I have never felt like that about any other place. However, the decision to fly out of India did make sense as it reduced the chance of illness, which had happened to me on my last visit and which I think may have influenced my decision and feelings this time around. Logically, I thought continuing my journey from Thailand would also improve my chances of cycling through Southeast Asia.

At Delhi Airport I had to remove Cynthia's front wheel and pedals and completely cover her in plastic wrap, so she looked like a mummy. As with every other flight I'd had so far, the ground crew were most helpful.

Chill out few days in Dubai with my former boss Jonathan, his wife Carol and their lovely kids.

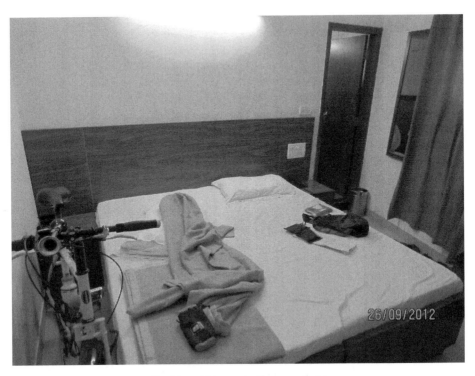

Cynthia and I in our double room – Delhi

11

THE EARLY DAYS

Time Again to Travel

Hunched over the computer, re-reading a draft report and making little progress, I sat back as a myriad of thoughts seemed to arrive in my middle-aged brain simultaneously. Where am I going? What do I want? What does the future hold? What's the meaning of life? And so on. Throughout my working life, I enjoyed work as a business appraiser, analysing how different businesses operated and performed. I had undertaken some interesting and intricate projects including the regeneration of Swansea waterfront, several marina developments around the country, and the valuation of a famous Newmarket Stable which was home to Enable, twice winner of the Arc. On site, while interviewing clients I was often impressed with their enthusiasm and motivation for their chosen way of life.

They had that spark, that 'get up and go' that drives entrepreneurs to the next level. It was so refreshing to experience the positivity they generated. I had no such ambitions within the company, largely because, although the work was often interesting, I wasn't so committed that I wanted to sell my soul for a Directorship, even if one was in the offing. I always preferred to keep things at an arm's length so that I could control them.

Looking back on my early career, I had had a crack at climbing the greasy pole in the corporate world. I worked long hours and left later or at the same time as the boss, I entertained clients late at night in bars and pole dancing clubs and encountered all the backstabbing that went on. I could never find it within myself to suck up to the boss the way some did, 'playing the game' as it was called, I preferred to let the quality of my work do the talking. That was fine to a point, but not the smartest move!

What were my options? I enjoyed a fairly independent lifestyle, working mainly from home and in charge of my own workload. So long as the reports were in on time and were of the appropriate quality, I was largely left alone to arrange appointments and get on with things. This work environment suited me well and I was fortunate enough to return to it on subsequent occasions throughout my life when needed. Something though was missing; the buzz, that indefinable something that many of my clients possessed and I was looking for.

I had no family ties, Nick was in his final year at Leeds and had achieved a First in Geography, something which I took full credit for! I was in need of a personal challenge and had an epiphany moment. I thought 'I am only on this earth once, as far as I know, so the quality of life and experience it offers should be grasped with both hands. Not everyone was in such a fortunate position or would necessarily have wanted to throw all vestiges of security up in the air. But such decisions never worried me.

I realised that my restless spirit had not gone away. Once more I took the decision to park the career and pick up a rucksack. In 2006, I sold my house and headed to Australia and New Zealand for three months. I decided to continue travelling and flew to South America where I backpacked for a further eleven months, travelling throughout Chile, Argentina, Brazil, Bolivia, Peru, Ecuador, and the Galapagos islands. It was a truly momentous journey.

There was so much to record. While in New Zealand I traversed the Franz Josef Glacier. Our guide cut steps into the ice, we clambered over and through narrow precipices, some less than a foot wide, with a 30-metre vertical drop or more to one side. On some sections we used ropes and we slid through a narrow ice tunnel that had a drop of fifteen feet. At the bottom was a collection of melted water that we ended up in. We crab-like clawed our way uphill on the other side and came back out onto the ice flow, feet first and soaking wet. On the North Island at Paihia I skydived from 12,000 feet. Looking down at the Islands in freefall, I thought that if things didn't go well at least I had a nice view to finish off with! It was a simply amazing experience.

In Pucón, Chile, I joined a group to climb an active volcano known as Volcan Villarrica. At 7,000 feet high its last eruption had occurred in 1984. The city had lost twenty-five people in its worst eruption, in 1971. Having been hiking and walking for some time. I had become quite fit. It took five hours to ascend the volcano over mixed terrain including scree, stones, snow and ice. Even though I was by far the oldest in the group, I reached the summit first, much to the surprise of our guide. We remained at the summit for an hour or so and walked around the crater. Looking over the edge and trying to dodge the sulphur fumes, I could see molten lava bubbling away in the crater about 200 metres below. Several climbers had apparently slipped over the edge. The views across the Andes towards Argentina were stunning, with numerous peaks and active volcanoes protruding above the mists. Volcan Villarrica was well worth the climb.

Like many of the large cities in South America, La Paz had a reputation for petty crime and a degree of violence. I had a small rucksack stolen from a table where I was having coffee. I was distracted for an instant, then when I turned around it was gone. It happened so quickly. I really was robbed in the blink of an eye. Fortunately, nothing was taken of value or that could not be replaced.

Life in the Andean Altiplano was harsh. For those not used to the altitude it could do strange things. Dizziness and sickness were the most common reactions but, once acclimatised they disappeared. In the more severe cases hallucinations and night wanderings could occur. My mate Rob who flew out to Lima to join me to do the Lares Trail to Machu Picchu fell foul with altitude sickness and I had to haul him back into the tent one night and leave the flaps open in -6 degrees. He didn't know where he was or what he was doing. Fortunately, he recovered in time for us to reach Machu Picchu. The indigenous population, sparse as it was, lived hand to mouth, on subsistence farming. There was no Government handouts or NHS equivalents. Birth mortality in the Bolivian Altiplano was about 40%, although if they could survive that, they could reach a good age, often living into the 90's. Natural medications were all around. Coca leaves were chewed as part of the regular diet. The leaves were said to ward off illnesses to the lungs and throat. Mosses were eaten and fused with hot water to protect the liver and stomach and so on. Most of us carried coca leaves to chew, which also helped protect against the effects of altitude sickness.

The Lares Trail took four days to complete. I hiked to the maximum height of 15.000ft, before entering the sun gate of Machu Picchu before dawn. Once inside we were able to watch the sunrise, although only those of us who had completed the Lares Trail, or the Machu Picchu Trail were entitled to enter at dawn. We enjoyed three hours of solitude and took in the majesty of what lay before us, before the hoards arrived by train. Machu Picchu took my breath away. Words could not describe it. Without question it instantly became my favourite place in the world. The vista was stunning, producing a mystical atmosphere and a complete sense of wonderment.

Having soaked up the atmosphere, four of us decided to climb Huayna Picchu which formed the sugar loaf peak at the back of Machu Picchu. Because the track was so steep and narrow, the number of people permitted to climb it at any one time was limited to 400. The peak was 800 feet high and the record for the climb was 22 minutes. We did it in 50. Close to the top we had to crawl through two caves, which were very narrow indeed. At one point, close to the peak, the dirt path was about a foot wide from a sheer vertical drop of almost 8,000 feet, that looked down to the Urubamba River below. There was an annual mortality of between six and fifteen people, who either fell off the edge or died leaping from one narrow section to the next, there was no protection. So far that year, six people had not made the return trip! The views from the top were spectacular.

On my return from South America in 2007 I was fortunate to pick up where I left off in my professional work, but this broadened to include working under contract overseas in the UAE (2007-2008) and Kazakhstan (2010-2012). I booked a flight to Dubai in 2007 and visited on spec and cold called surveying/valuing practices; without too much difficulty I landed a position in Abu Dhabi. At that time, it was the peak of a property boom and it was common to witness numerous *'dishdashas'* enter a building to conclude a deal on an undeveloped area of sand situated on somewhere like Reem Island. They would return from the building and pass a piece of paper to another *'dishdash'* in the car park, concluding in a quick 'turnkey' of the property plus 10%. It was all quite open and quite normal.

Coincidentally, Nick moved to Abu Dhabi at the same time as me. After finishing his degree, he landed a job with Etihad Airways and spent several months undergoing a training programme. We were able to spend most weekends together and I enjoyed our regular catch-ups. Then the 2008 financial crash suddenly hit with a vengeance. The car parks and land around Dubai airport were littered with Ferraris, BMW's and all manner of marque cars, with the keys left in the ignition as ex-pats caught the first available flight out of town. Somewhat too late fencing was erected, apparently to hide the exodus that was taking place. I had no such baggage, however I was made redundant and with no chance of work anywhere else I returned to the UK. I was somewhat disappointed as I had enjoyed the work, the people and Abu Dhabi itself. I had preferred it over Dubai as it was more of a contained city. Dubai was a sprawl with many centres linked by road. It had also virtually run out of oil, whereas Abu Dhabi had the money as it was sitting on reserves that would be around for another hundred years. Looking ahead, it remained to be seen how valuable the reserves would be with the green revolution taking hold. There were of course many countries which would continue to be reliant upon fossil fuels for way beyond the time limits set by some Western politicians.

In 2010 I found my way to Kazakhstan, which proved a complete contrast. I answered an advertisement in the RICS magazine and was interviewed in London by a top bloke, he was much younger than me although we got on immediately. Living and working in an ex-Soviet state was an education. The Kazakhs were great, certainly the ones I met and especially the women who were very efficient and quite gorgeous. Our office resembled a fashion house as Steve, the boss, preferred to employ attractive women on the basis that if you had a bad day, at least the office provided a positive environment. Kazakhstan was a very male dominant society, and Steve was as keen as possible to appoint as much female talent in the office as he could. He certainly succeeded. I was instructed to value an amazing array of railway trucks, rail yards, industrial and commercial property together with sea going flat bottom boats in the Caspian. Trying to marry the western way of valuation with the former Soviet way proved immensely difficult, and many lively discussions ensued with the local valuers, but with a bit of give and take and understanding, we invariably reached an amicable conclusion on most occasions.

I lived in a modern flat on the 22nd floor of a glass building in Almaty. The views were amazing and overlooked the snow-capped Tien Shan mountain range, which was an offshoot of the Himalayas which separated China and Kyrgyzstan. Almaty lay on a fault line and it did not disappoint. When Nick visited from Abu Dhabi, while still working for Etihad, we were having breakfast one morning when the building shook for several seconds and we both lost our balance in the room. It was a close shave, a 6.3 quake hit and fortunately for us, the building remained intact, otherwise we would probably have spent far too much time removing glass from our anatomy.

After spending just over a year in Kazakhstan, I decided to call it a day and return to England. Sitting on the British Midland flight home I rapidly concluded that I would see my working life out as painlessly as possible. I knew at my age there was no such thing as a career path, that path had effectively run dry at forty, but I could still offer a specialised skill set. On returning to England, I recharged the batteries by hiking the whole South-West Coast Path from Minehead to Studland/Poole. I completed 1000km in six weeks and two days. The hike certainly rejuvenated the mind and body and armed with refreshed vigour I approached my former company, and once again began appraisal work in the West Country.

Ice tunnelling in the Franz Joseph Glacier

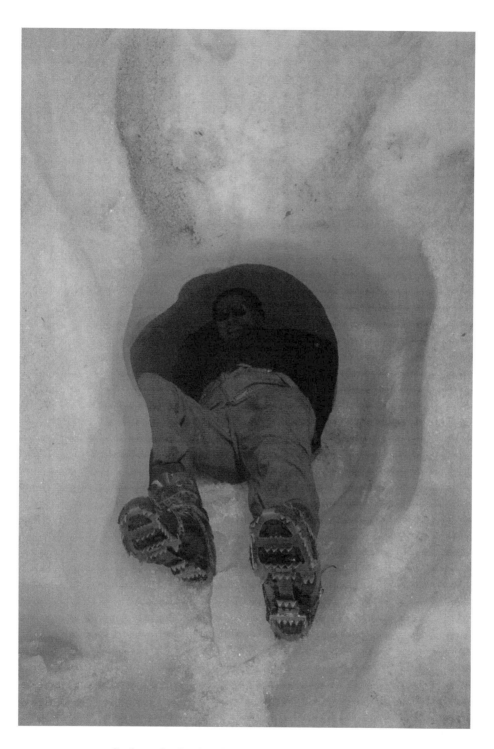

Coming up feet first through an ice tunnel - Franz Joseph glacier

Nothing like a lungful of sulphur! Volcan Villarica, Chile

Iguazu Falls, Argentina

The Tree Rock, Bolivia

Salt hotel, Salar De Uyuni, Bolivia. Just need the chips!

Away changing rooms, Bolivia

Machu Picchu from the summit of Huayna Picchu

Top of Huayna Picchu, some climb!

A few of us on the Lares Trail to Machu Picchu at 15,000 ft

Rob and I doing what we do best near Cuzco, Peru

12

AND SO WE MOVE ON

The Final Leg

I left India with a heavy heart. It had been described in one of the Lonely Planet books as the most colourful country in the world, I wish I could have agreed. I had tried to embrace the colour and culture but failed dismally. Bangkok on the other hand was a great city, vibrant and full of character and places to visit. The numerous air-conditioned malls met and ran alongside the covered street vendors by the roadside. It was a blend that worked. It was a pleasure wandering through the street stalls. The vendors gave me no hassle, so I felt comfortable looking and buying. I replenished items that had been left behind, broken, damaged or worn out. The street food was also great. I didn't get the chance to try it in India, as I was too busy avoiding the touts. Bangkok was also cheap. My hotel, selected from Lonely Planet, was ideal and charged thirteen pounds a night. It was only a couple of quid more than Delhi but believe me, there was no comparison. Bangkok was a great place to take time to plan for the next move. I picked up a selection of maps and chose my preferred route. The first part would take me north east through Thailand to Laos where I'd cross at Vientiane and head north to Luang Prabang. I'd then head back south following the Mekong into Cambodia and onto Vietnam. There was a cycle route along the Mekong Delta which I also wanted to incorporate into my route. People I had spoken to raved about Laos and Cambodia, well the entire Southeast Asian area got a big thumbs up.

I had to hole up in Bangkok for a little while longer, as a typhoon was due to hit, and a lot of rain was expected. The storm delay provided the opportunity to give Cynthia a major scrub up and overhaul after the flight. The hotel kindly allowed me to undertake this work adjacent to the main entrance. She had come out relatively unscathed and I felt that was due in no small measure to Thorn's quality of build; the bike was superb. I also took the opportunity to bulk up on calories. The hotel did a particularly excellent breakfast buffet. Bacon and eggs with tomato, pancakes, egg fried rice, maple syrup and ketchup on the same plate does amazing things for your tastebuds.

As I set out for Laos, I took a somewhat circuitous route out of Bangkok. I came back onto the main road, known as highway 2, which led to the Thai-Lao Friendship Bridge. It was a busy route that was made up mainly of two and three carriageways, although you could easily filter off these roads and access any decent sized town or city. This meant I could stop and shop safely and re-join the main road a little further on. There was also a full width shoulder lane for cyclists and motorcycles, which was a real luxury. I had never seen a nation of such spontaneous smilers. They were all at it and it was impossible not to smile back. Whenever I stopped for something to eat at a roadside cook up, they kindly invited me in. The street food was pretty good, I stuck to the hot stuff and BBQ duck was a favourite (at least I thought it was duck)! The birds were smaller than in the UK and the locals had this quaint ritual of battering them until they resembled a pancake. There were plenty of dislocated bones to navigate around, but the food was OK nonetheless.

Immediately having left the outskirts of Bangkok, the topography became flat. There were wetland areas where I saw numerous snakes, light yellow in colour, and a huge lizard which must have been three or four feet long. It was black with bright green striations down its back. The further north I went, the landscape turned agricultural and semi-tropical. Monkeys would swing around telegraph poles and wires. From a cyclist's perspective it was ideal as there were no hills at all and always something to see. The downside was the high humidity, which was tough to deal with. Within five minutes of setting off, I was soaked in sweat, literally rivers of the stuff seeped down the side of my head, down my body and legs and into my feet. I had to stop regularly, every half-an-hour, to replenish liquid. Fortunately, there were plenty of opportunities in the numerous towns and villages along the way to fill up. Dehydration and exercise didn't exactly compliment the malaria tablets I was taking but with a bit of judicious shifting as to when I took my tablet, I felt much better.

The route through Thailand wasn't the most scenic, however, the people made up for it and it was always a pleasure to stop and spend a few minutes with them at the roadside. I tried to do this most of the time, however the need for a few minutes of air conditioning proved too much of a temptation on some occasions. I would stop off at a 7-Eleven or, would you believe it, a Tesco Lotus (it must have taken the marketing boys at Tesco a few sleepless nights to come up with that one). Accommodation in Thailand, and across Southeast Asia, was cheap. I stayed in hotels of various quality, although all were ok. In the smaller towns, there were rarely any hotels advertised, as they went under the name of Resorts, which could mean a few chalet style units tucked away behind the town or on the periphery. Approaching the Laos border, I crossed at the Friendship Bridge, which lay some 22km east of the capital Vientiane. I had no problems at the border, and it was a seamless transfer from Thailand into Laos. The visa and checks took around thirty minutes and could not have been easier.

I had downloaded the Lonely Planet guide onto my Kindle which, apart from my phone, was the best thing I had put in my pannier. After securing accommodation for my stay, I was able to take in the city. It was quiet, Vientiane only had a population of 700,000, but it was a very attractive city, full of character displaying the legacy of French colonialism. The architecture and street signs had French imprint, which was very stylish. The city was home to historic temples and monuments, including a statue of the former king; King Fa Ngum, who stood in commanding posture overlooking the Mekong River. The centrepiece of the city was the Avenue Lane Xang that extended from the Presidential Palace (which itself overlooked the Mekong) north to the Victory Monument which was built in 1957 (although it looked older). The Avenue itself was broadly the equivalent of Pall Mall or Whitehall, with many of the Ministries and major financial institutions along either side.

A habit, to mark my arrival in a new country, had been to celebrate with a few beers, it became a sort of good luck charm. I found a 4th floor bar overlooking the Mekong and watched the sun go down, it was just beautiful. There was something about the light which distinguished Southeast Asia from anywhere else, just as the light in Dubai and Abu Dhabi had mirrored the Middle East. I reflected and counted myself as one of the most fortunate human beings on the planet to be able to see such sights and incredible places, good and bad. The sunset was a superb introduction to Laos. The French of course, were all over Indochina like a rash and who could blame them. Given the choice between

Indochina and India (incorporating Pakistan as was) I knew which I preferred, and which would get my vote; the French were not daft. Coincidently, I watched a BBC World News item during my stay where they interviewed the Indian housing minister about the problems facing Delhi. With the increased wealth people were pouring into the city looking for work, they calculated that 1,000 cars a day were being added to the roads. The minister believed high rise buildings were the answer, whilst the opposition wanted to keep the city low rise and green. Well over four million people were living in slums according to the report and having lived off the land, I could not see them settling in a box on the 20th floor somewhere! That, I thought, would take some persuasion.

Cuisine in Laos was sensational. Traditional French and Asian fare offered just about everything. They had a place called Jomo Bakery which did all day American breakfasts, unbelievable waffles with maple syrup and cream. It was just the most sublime way to start the day.

The Laos flag consisted of three horizontal bars: a central blue band (incorporating a white centrally positioned circle) and red bands on either side. They also flew another flag, all red with a hammer and sickle. The full name for Laos was the People's Democratic Republic which could be interpreted in a number of ways, however the meaning of the flag was supposed to highlight 'work'. The interpretation seemed to be something of a grey area, but from what little

I had seen, and from what the locals said, those on lower incomes did get looked after and that was clearly evident. It appeared that the poorest region in Laos was to the east, bordering with Vietnam. The reason for the poverty, was that farmers could not grow enough rice to sustain the community for the whole year since they could not expand their agricultural holdings. This was due to the danger from unexploded ordnance (Laos was effectively carpet bombed during the Vietnam war). The whole Indochina region had similar warnings, and since arriving a number of people had warned me not to go cycling 'off-piste' so to speak. The advice was to stick to the main roads at all times.

I decided to catch a bus to Luang Prabang, leaving Cynthia at my hotel in Vientiane, as the terrain was all mountainous. Luang Prabang was a small town, it had a population of around 25,000 and was situated some 300+km north of Vientiane. It could have been a whole world away. Access was by bus or plane, the latter costed around US$90 whereas the bus was a lot cheaper. It took ten hours and followed a series of 'S' bends pretty much from start to finish. Most visitors took the bus; three left Vientiane every day during my stay. I imagined more might be scheduled during high season (from November to February), coinciding with the more temperate climate.

Luang Prabang was like nowhere else I had visited. It was a gem that unfortunately had been discovered and would undoubtedly become a backpackers' favourite, well it was getting that way already. The bus ride up was full of highs, and I was glad to have travelled in daylight. It was a joy to see the unbelievable mountain formations rising from the jungle. Vertical rock and sugar loaves in all directions formed an almost unique vista. It looked like something out of Jurassic Park and, to be honest, if I had seen brachiopods grazing, they wouldn't have felt out of place. The mountain villages were quite isolated although each formed their own community at the roadside. Most had a school which kids cycled to and from, holding umbrellas for extra shade. It looked like something out of Mary Poppins. All the kids wore uniform, and all were very smart, which given the dust and the washing facilities was something. Each village had a shop and, as evening drew on, everyone headed to the communal washing area (a stream or pond) and, after washing, they all trooped back to the village together. There was a real sense of community, people ate together and looked after each other. Each village seemed to have communal washing lines and a harvest of red chillies drying on cloths or on tin bowls that looked like dustbin lids. There was a serenity about the Lao people, they smiled, always said hello and were delighted when you took an interest in their produce. The whole way of life avoided confrontation. I was sure that if I had shouted or argued or showed any form of verbal aggression, they would not have known what to do. They were lovely people. What surprised me, both travelling through Lao and in Luang Prabang itself, was the apparent quality of life. The village properties were built of cane or brick, and I had not seen any beggars since arriving in the country. All around was lush broad-leafed vegetation, that rose out from a mountainous landscape.

There weren't enough superlatives to describe Luang Prabang itself. Nestled beside the Mekong river, the town featured some wonderful colonial architecture and heritage. It was a UNESCO site so while growth would undoubtedly occur, I hoped that it would keep its character (I wasn't holding my breath). The locals knew the place was about to explode onto the tourist map in a big way. The tour operators and tuk-tuk drivers already had the well-worn tourist phrases in English and were targeting every westerner or non-Lao that passed. There were a lot of guest houses, all of which appeared really well maintained, plus temples and markets and a shed load of bars and restaurants in town and along the river. Having a cold beer and watching the sunset on the river was a real pleasure.

Luang Prabang was gearing up for the season, so the sound of hammering was never far away. There were only two main streets, one inland and the other along the Mekong, each was linked by a series of narrow streets mostly with guest houses. The vegetation was colourful, the town was very clean, and it was a delight just to wander aimlessly around it at leisure. From the town, you could take a variety of tours to see waterfalls, or trek. A couple of days was enough to get a good feel for the town itself. There were loads of places to hire cycles and motorbikes to explore further. I was sure the town would change as more visitors put it on their itinerary. I had heard that China intended to build a railway through Laos to Vientiane which supposedly would link with Luang Prabang. I hoped the rumour would not come to pass, as I couldn't imagine the character would remain the same. As with all Laos, there was a very relaxed atmosphere in the town. Beyond the river was the jungle canopy which extended down to the water's edge. Beyond that were the mountain ranges which seemed to curve around, enclosing the whole town. It was beautiful. I could see why people called it Shangri La, it must have been pretty close to it, and I think the locals had woken up to this. I just hoped the balance stayed so that visitors in years to come could feel the same sensation about the town.

I was sorry to leave Luang Prabang, but I knew that there was so much ahead. Originally it had been my intention to cycle through Laos into Cambodia. On a closer inspection of the map, I realised there was only one road border crossing into Cambodia and after that I would have had to cycle south (almost to the Vietnam border) before backtracking to Siem Reap and Angkor Wat. Then I would have had to cycle back south again to reach the capital city Phnom Penh. So, instead of doing a zig zag tour, I decided to cycle to Udon Thani, which lay inside the Thai border (and was about 100km from Vientiane), and planned to catch a sleeper train back to Bangkok. It meant that I could continue eastwards towards Cambodia, and the cycle to Laos became an offshoot so to speak.

I passed through the Laos/Thai customs in ten minutes, it was unbelievably quick. Wearing a football shirt seemed to do it for just about every border post. The customs officials loved to talk about English football. This was the same with the military and police in every country I had visited. Officials generally became so helpful once they knew what I was doing. I hoped for it to continue, as it had helped me out on more than one occasion.

I arrived in Bangkok at 7am having enjoyed a sound sleep on the train. Upon my arrival I managed to lug Cynthia off the train, which was no mean feat given that the height of the carriage was well above the platform and the carriage doors were not exactly wide. In the main concourse I filled up on coffee and doughnuts and tried to work out how to get out of the city. Eventually, after completing a circuit of sorts which took me almost four hours, I got onto the right road. My navigation skills were suspect, I freely admit, but it didn't help that three roads were all numbered the same as the one I thought I wanted. Regardless, it all sorted out eventually and I got to know my way around east Bangkok reasonably well.

The distance between Bangkok and Poi Pet (Thai/ Cambodia border) was about three days of comfortable cycling. Mind you, in the humidity it was hard to rack up the mileage. I had improved from a pathetic 60km per day, from when I first started cycling in Thailand heading to Laos, to a more respectable 100km per day. I must have been getting conditioned to the humidity however my progress didn't alter the fact that cycling conditions were not ideal. At least the malaria tablets settled, which was a real plus.

The topography to the Thai border was flat, comprised of wetlands and rice paddies, interspersed by numerous villages and towns. Fortunately, the towns were evenly spaced for each day's cycling. On my last night I held up three kilometres from the border at Aranyaprathet and set off early the following morning to cross at Poi Pet. Like all land border crossings the whole place was bustling with markets, taxis and people wanting to take me here there and everywhere for a cheap price! On the Thai side they had a scam where they sold fake Cambodian visas, tourists would then have to pay again at Cambodian immigration. It was a bit naughty and I was thankful that Lonely Planet had highlighted it. I was approached and politely told them where to go, despite their insistence that without their help I would not get into Cambodia! Nice try fellers but no lollypop! Crossing the border was dead easy, I just followed a dirt road along with loads of others, passing casinos and hotels in-between, which looked like real dens of iniquity. I sorted the visa for Cambodia which costed US$20 and it took ten minutes for officials to validate my passport. The immigration officer was insistent that he had to look at Cynthia, just to see her and sound her klaxon. The klaxon proved quite a hit with the locals and often when I was in a shop, I could hear it sound off as a result of local kids having gathered around. I had heard the Cambodian Visa was a good one to get, as it was very colourful and artistic which it proved to be.

After clearing the border, I headed for Sisophon which was about 48km ahead. Like Thailand the road was pretty straight with a decent cycle shoulder, either side of which were rice paddies, irrigated by numerous streams and rivers. At either side of the road were rice paddies, which were irrigated by numerous streams and rivers. The locals fished in these, casting their nets into the water. These places were also a magnet for kids who jumped and swam in the often muddy waters. In fact, thinking about it, most kids I saw were always up to their necks in water. Unlike Thailand, which offered frequent petrol stations with either 7-Eleven's or Tesco Lotus convenience stores, Cambodia had very little. If I wanted a drink, I pulled up roadside at a village where many of the shops were effectively extensions of local dwellings. The 'shops' would usually be tin roof shacks, with dusty floors and a sleeping area. To the front would be a display of rustic shelving with limited stock and a large red ice box where the drinks were kept. Very few places had a proper upright chiller, consequently the drinks weren't that cold. A bloke in a lorry came by and delivered ice slabs, which he would cut with a saw from a six-foot by one-foot section. He'd then place the cut ice slabs into the red box. I loved stopping at these places, I did it often as it gave me a chance to say hello whilst putting a dollar or two into the local shopkeepers' pockets. Without exception, when I stopped to buy something, a lady would bring out a chair for me to sit in the shade. The locals really were so courteous and charming. I always made a big deal about thanking them.

All along the way the kids would wave and shout hello as they passed by on motor scooters, their smiles would melt any heart. Cute didn't do them justice. The few who knew a little English came to talk to me. They were truly something and very inquisitive. Almost without exception every dwelling had a tv which would be on all day. Most households also seemed to own a scooter. They were real pieces of work and used for just about everything. Few wore crash helmets, and it was not unusual to see mum, dad and up to three kids astride a 125cc Honda. The best sight was when the bikes were used to transport stuff. I saw one bike loaded with four sacks, which I reckoned were eight-feet wide and at least six-feet high, the rider was all over the place. The scooters even carried livestock and you would often see two full sized dead pigs strapped on the back, with their trotters in the air. They also had a cunning version of a trailer, designed for whatever task was needed, again for livestock or pallets of goods.

I cycled from Sisophon to Siem Reap (about 110km) and arrived at around 2 pm. The tourist office found me an excellent place to stay for US$12 which had breakfast included. On my way into the city, scooters came alongside Cynthia and the drivers welcomed and chatted to me. They had no ulterior motive and were just being friendly. Siem Reap was a city about the size of Exeter and from the direction I entered, the first impression was definitely that of a tourist city. I cycled down what I called 'the strip' with large well-appointed hotels on either side, then I hit the centre which laid claim to some attractive French colonial architecture. The main hub of activity was focused on the Old Market where there was a proliferation of bars, restaurants, massage parlours and shops. It was backpacker country and close to where my hotel was.

People came to Siem Reap for one reason, to see Angkor Wat. The complex of temples lay about five kilometres to the north and after purchasing a ticket en route I was free to go and explore. Needless to say, there were motorbikes to hire, bikes with carriage trailers, limos, buses; a whole myriad of transportation made its way from Siem Reap to Angkor like ants. I enjoyed cycling and taking my time. I would meander along, stop off, check out the various temples, enjoy a beer or two. It was a great way of seeing an amazing piece of history and architecture. Angkor, which was the main temple, meant Capital City and was the capital of the Khmer empire that existed in the area between the 9th and 12th centuries. At its height more than one million people lived there. The size of the site was several kilometres square and you wouldn't walk it. Although Angkor Wat was the temple everyone knew, it was not my personal favourite. Bayon and some of the smaller temples were more interesting and visually impressive. If I had been a keen historian, I would have wanted to spend weeks in the temple complex. However, I was not one. I liked to focus on the impact of the vista, how it affected me when I saw it and the setting of a place. To me, that was the wow factor I suppose. That's me being a superficial kind of bloke when it comes to history. I want to know about general history but not overturn every stone, if you see what I mean. Angkor Wat did have a wonderful setting and was wrapped around by a lake moat. I travelled through woodland on well surfaced roads that took me around the magnificent complex.

I spent a full day sightseeing and for me that was sufficient. It was strange riding Cynthia without panniers, and it was the first time I'd done so since leaving England. I nearly fell off when Cynthia's front spun round. She was so light and responsive. I was used to handling the equivalent of a tank. I thought I'd see what she could do on the flat and there was a straight stretch of 1.3km between temples. I managed to keep at or above 30km/h for the entire length and felt quite pleased as she was still a lump, even when stripped of all panniers. She was certainly no sleek machine.

It was time for me to leave Siem Reap, I decided to catch a ferry across the water to Battambang as I'd heard it was worth seeing. If it had been the height of the monsoon season, I could have taken a ferry direct to Phnom Penh, but the detour across Lake Tonlé Sap didn't bother me. The ferry was smaller than I had envisaged. Seating along either side allowed for about twenty people and bikes were lashed to the roof. I had decided to make the six-hour crossing between the two cities, because it was a welcome change from chewing dust and ingesting fumes from vehicles. The ferry was full and as the journey progressed, it was evident why the boat was the size and shape it was. Vegetation almost enveloped us at many points and some very careful navigation was needed to avoid the propellers becoming jammed up. In between the dense jungle were open tracts of water and numerous lake villages. The buildings were either floating or precariously perched on stilts. The ferry provided a vital lifeline for locals travelling between these villages and if householders didn't possess a boat, they were effectively isolated. Villagers would be rowed out and would clamber aboard. You could see why the ferry didn't run all year round because even at the end of the monsoon season, which I was in, water levels in certain places were very shallow.

It was a welcome change taking the ferry and a great way to spend a day. Most of the passengers were tourists and there was quite a large Dutch contingent, which was good as invariably they were always good company. The ferry dropped us off in the centre of Battambang city on the west bank. Accommodation was easy to find and plentiful.

I stayed in a small hotel on the east bank next to the large Kings Hotel. It was very new, and the room overlooked the river which I thought was pretty excellent for US$12 a night. The Royal was a backpacker's favourite and good value too. Coincidentally, I bumped into two of the Dutch couples from the ferry who happened to be eating at the same place as me. They very kindly invited me over and one couple, Judith and Roel, invited me over to their hotel on their last night for dinner. They were a delightful couple and were superb company. A real highlight for me in Battambang was the Gecko café, which believe me was as good as it gets. Situated close to the city centre, it occupied the first floor of a French colonial building and had an open seating area on two sides. It had a very welcoming atmosphere and the food, especially breakfast, was sensational. The atmosphere was created by the staff, all girls who were a real delight, very friendly and spoke English. They were all employed because they had families to support, and on the back of the menu there was a small CV for each girl explaining her background and intentions. Believe me, if you could have transferred these girls to any hotel or catering establishment in the UK people would have queued at the door to get in. Another good place to eat was Éves Cafe on the waterfront, which did great pancakes as well.

Mandi, a very good friend of mine from England, who I met and travelled with while walking the South West Coastal Path, had volunteered in Battambang and I took the opportunity to look up where she worked. CCT or Cambodian Children's Trust had been set up a few years ago by a young Australian and she continued to be very involved. I met the local manager and a couple of the volunteers. The trust looked after some three hundred children, the majority of whom attended school. It collected children of all ages from parents who were unable to fully look after them for a variety of social reasons. Having attended the trust or school, they were then returned to their parents in the evening so that the parental bond was maintained. The trust also supported scholarships for more able children to give them a chance to develop their education, which was so vital. I learned that many children, once they reached a certain academic standard, left school and returned to their families to teach their siblings rather than continuing to pursue a career. I noticed that most of the volunteer sector was supported by either Australians or Americans.

My purpose for visiting Battambang was twofold. Firstly, to apply for a Vietnamese Visa in advance which was a prerequisite to visit Vietnam. I thought it might be easier to get one in Battambang than in Phnom Penh. My second reason was that cycling to Phnom Penh looked easier from Battambang than from Siem Reap and there were larger towns on the way which were more likely to provide accommodation. My initial visit to the Vietnam Consulate lasted about twenty minutes and entailed completion of the usual form. I explained to the official that I wanted a three-month visa as I was cycling, and it would save having to make a sudden pit stop to Saigon or Hanoi to renew. Had I only wanted a one-month visa, which was the usual length granted, I think they could have provided it on the same day but because I wanted a longer visa, they asked if I would mind returning the following day. This I did, and good on them, they granted the three-month visa which of course I paid more for, but ultimately, it would save me a lot of hassle later down the line. They could not have been more helpful. The Consul himself came out to present me with the visa and said he hoped I enjoyed cycling through their country. It was a nice touch.

It took three days to cycle the 293km to Phnom Penh. There was an even space of towns in between, and I stopped at Pursat and Kampong Cham. The road was dusty although most of the way there was a decent shoulder lane. This was just as well since the seemingly mild mannered people, once behind a ton and a half of metal transformed into Sebastian Vettel! The worst offenders were the taxis (all Toyota Camrys), mini-buses and 4x4's. These guys hurtled down the middle of the road, horns blaring continuously as they tried to cover the distance between Battambang and the capital in record time. I witnessed some near misses with cattle that frequently wandered across the road and also village children. The aforementioned group appeared to accelerate as they passed through! There were numerous villages and cycling through I witnessed the poverty, yet always, people, and the kids especially, shouted hello and waved. I always returned the greeting even though after several hours on the road, it wore a bit thin. It wasn't much to ask, if these kids got a buzz out of it then responding wasn't so hard. I reckon that if I had a dollar for every "hello" and wave I had given over that three-day period, I could have afforded to fly first class around the world and still have enough left to stay in a five-star beachfront hotel in the West Indies.

Cycling afforded me the opportunity to connect with the villagers, who would chat while passing by on scooters or in shops when I stopped to buy a drink. I used to stop regularly and pour cans of sugary drinks down my throat due to the heat and constant sugar rush needed. I was invited, well more like directed, to two homes where I spent half an hour or so meeting the families and exchanging some very basic English. The Cambodians were so welcoming, it would have been difficult not to be sociable as the people (of all ages) were so friendly and genuinely approachable. How could I not smile when three girls on a scooter passed, waved, and said hello, or, when a feller on a scooter loaded with some produce in the most bizarre fashion passed me with a smile. The humidity really took it out of me. I found my recovery time took quite a bit longer, but at least I was still achieving the distance I had set myself.

Phnom Penh was a rapidly transforming city with a population of about one and a half million. As with most cities, the periphery was dominated by the poorer people. In fact, the whole area seemed to reflect a self-contained marketplace for them, with every kind of activity imaginable available, including shops for building materials, repair workshops, welding, cafes and more. The dwellings fronted onto a dusty shoulder which invariably became wind born as lorries and vehicles veered onto the stretches to avoid oncoming traffic. The areas bustled with people and a million tuk-tuk drivers. Traffic flow was what you made it, there were no rules as such, well there didn't seem to be, at any given point of the road. Vehicles, tuk-tuks and scooters converged from all directions, weaving their way in and out. This occurred in the city centre, so it was a well-tried method. The city centre was a changing face. There was a mix of early 20th century French colonial architecture, 1960s Khmer buildings, ornate gold leaf temples and the Royal Palace. It was a fascinating blend, which I suppose summed up the people. Many of the older colonial properties had not been properly maintained and had fallen into some state of disrepair. I understood that a lot of the buildings were being acquired by hoteliers and converted into quality boutique hotels. It reflected the greater demand generated by tourism and showed the city's ongoing development as a commercial and business centre. It was good to see the fast-flowing Mekong River again. The river bisected the city and had helped it become an important port. It seemed strange that only a few weeks ago, I was watching the river flow some 1,500km to the north at Luang Prabang. It was a bit like meeting an old friend. In truth, the river at the central point of the city was an extension of the lake but it was classed as a river.

The west bank was where the lifeblood of the city existed. The tourist hub extended along Sisowath Quay with numerous hotels, hostels, restaurants, tour offices and of course millions of tuk-tuk drivers who consistently invited me for the trip of my life! I suppose from a tourist perspective, the place to visit was the Foreign Correspondents Club or, as it was known, the FCC. This distinctive colonial building overlooked the Mekong and, on the first and second floors, you could sit watching the sunset with some liquid refreshment between 5pm and 7pm (happy hour). The FCC was the place where foreign correspondents collected during the 1970s, particularly when the Khmer Rouge and Pol Pot played such a part in the country's recent tainted history.

Second only to Angkor Wat, were the Killing Fields and S21. A visit to both was a must to understand the country's darkest period of history and its response to what happened. It seemed unbelievable that the events only took place in the 1970s, effectively shutting out Cambodia from the whole world. The Choeung Ek Genocidal Center (or as tourists knew it as the Killing Fields) was situated about 15km from the city centre. A tuk-tuk was the best way of getting there. It was essential to wear a face mask on the way since the airborne dirt and dust was quite something. The entrance was low key and accessed down a drive. For US$5 I got hooked up to an excellent audio set and could subsequently wander to the sequential markers at my leisure, listening to the history of the site and personal tales from survivors and the guards.

Pol Pot imposed his doctrine of democratic communism during the mid-1970s until 1978. He was the son of a wealthy family and studied in France. He didn't attain his degree but spent most of his time with the French Communist Party. On his return to Cambodia he became a teacher, which was something of an irony as many of those murdered by his regime were teachers. He instigated a policy of no education, obedience to the party, work and revolution, with unbelievable violence. As with many dictatorships, he created his red army from uneducated peasants, villagers and rural communities. He convinced youthful recruits to believe that they had a future under his rule. Teachers and professional classes of all description were rounded up, tortured and murdered. Throughout Cambodia there were believed to be some 300 killing fields, of which the one at Choeung Ek was considered to be the largest. Many of the others could not be touched because of unexploded ordnance from USA bombings that were dropped to prevent fuel lines to the Viet Kong. Walking around the Killing Fields, it was difficult to imagine the horror of what went on. The audio description was at times very graphic. At the time of my visit eighty-six of the one hundred and twenty-nine mass graves had been uncovered, accounting for almost 9,000 bodies of children and adults alike. The largest contained 450 bodies. Those that remained undisturbed were likely to stay that way to afford respect to the dead.

On the ground where the horrific deeds had taken place, I could see hollows where graves had been uncovered, and where, through the effluxion of time, the soil had moved. The single most graphic example of the cruelty was the Chankiri Tree, words failed me at this point. I just hung my head at the horror of what happened, it was where the red guards held the children (as young as babies) by their legs and feet and swung them so that their heads connected to the trunk. The brutality was unbelievable. The central feature, or edifice, within the Killing Fields was the Memorial Stupa where skulls and bones had been collected and displayed. The skulls were divided into sex and age groups. The museum also showed the tools used to kill. It was considered a waste to use bullets, so bludgeoning and hacking were the preferred methods of disposal.

Security Office 21 (S21) stood in the centre of Phnom Penh. It had been reclassified as a genocide museum after originally being designed for detention, interrogation, torture and killing. All detainees had been individually documented. Some 20,000 were tortured, killed or moved on to the Killing Fields. Again ironically, the building had originally been a school in the 1960s. As I walked into the cells, there were pictures of people and accounts of torture and confessions. It was truly dreadful. I wondered how such seemingly mild mannered people could be capable of such inhumanity. Then again, it only took a small number of 'focused' individuals appropriately motivated to instil sufficient fear and obedience across a population. It was happening all over the world. Over one quarter of the entire Cambodian population were murdered during this three-year period; it was a staggering statistic. Of course, not all the people involved were caught, and it was possible that some were still walking the streets. Something that was noticeable was the lack of old people around in comparison with other countries I'd visited. Cambodia had a lost generation. Furthermore, the trauma resulting from the madness caused many women's menstrual cycles to cease. As women stopped having children the population gap grew wider, encompassing both young and old generations. Arguably one of the worst and most incredible acts of world political decision making was the acceptance of the Khmer Rouge as a legitimate party by no less than the USA, UK, Australia, Germany and France. It handed the Khmer Rouge a seat and a voice at the UN! In the end, it was Vietnamese troops who came and toppled the brutal regime of Pol Pot and his Khmer Rouge. It was a sobering experience visiting the Killing Fields and S21 but fortunately the country had recovered, and I hoped that the land continued to smile in the future for all the right reasons.

It was time for me to move on from Cambodia and head to Vietnam. I had decided to take the ferry down the Mekong to the Delta region, to Chau Doc in Vietnam. It would once more save me from breathing in vast quantities of road dust! The boat ride was a six-hour trip and positioned me well for the cycle through the Mekong delta and towards my eventual destination which was Saigon. The ferry departed Phnom Penh at 8am and I travelled with some twenty backpackers who all had the same idea. The journey was fairly uneventful, the banks of the mighty river gave way to small waterside communities and agriculture. Occasionally larger watercrafts and freighters would pass, ploughing their way towards Phnom Penh. After three quarters of the journey was completed, we pulled into a muddy riverbank and climbed some steps. At the top, was a building that turned out to be the Cambodian checkpoint. I handed my passport in, had it stamped, and then got back on the boat which continued downstream to the Vietnamese border, where a similar pattern was repeated. It was the first river border crossing I had encountered and could not have been more straightforward.

Chau Doc was one of several large towns and communities located within the Mekong Delta. As a town, it didn't have a great deal to offer, but it was one of the busiest, especially with tourists, as it was the link to Cambodia and there was also a direct coach service to Saigon. After resting up in a somewhat basic hotel, the following morning I set off with Cynthia to cycle through the Delta region. A road sign read Hanoi 2,200km, so it was quite a cycle in prospect. The humidity was higher than I had experienced anywhere. In Thailand the temperature had remained at a constant 33 degrees. In Vietnam, within five minutes of setting out, I became a squelching mass, dripping in perspiration, which set the tone for every day after. Because of the high loss of fluid, I rarely, if ever, had to stop to splash my boots. The key was to get as much liquid down me as quickly as possible. Fortunately, there were many villages where I could stop for a drink. People's dwellings were mostly straw or timber in design, and many of them had a large ice box near the roadside. As soon as I saw one, I would pull in to be met by the owner who would entice me to select a can or two of whatever she had. In a day, particularly whilst travelling through the Delta region, I would consume sometimes five cans of red bull, plus cans of lemonade or coke or whatever high calorie sugar drink came to hand. As the day progressed, every part of my anatomy stuck to other bits. The constant sweat, friction and movement resulted in quite painful and uncomfortable raw areas across my body. Thank goodness for showers and Vaseline! After leaving Chau Doc, my first port of call was Sa Đéc. I then stopped off in Tân An before finally arriving in Saigon. The Delta region was characterised by an almost continuous number of villages and small towns. Many of the communities were set in small inlets surrounded by mangroves. The route also took me over numerous large bridges, beneath which were the tributaries of the Mekong. The scale of the Delta region was quite something.

I had heard that people had deliberately avoided Vietnam because of a certain reputation it had. After being in the country for only five days (not long I grant you to form a conclusive opinion) I felt confident to disregard any negative warnings about the place. The people were equally as friendly as any I had met in Southeast Asia. They were maybe not as vociferous as their Cambodian neighbours (but then no one would be on that scale) but I still got all the smiles and acknowledgements, and scooters would come alongside to chat and pat me on the back. Without question, the key was the way I was travelling. There was nothing wrong with backpackers, only a handful of years ago I had backpacked through Australia, New Zealand and South America for the best part of fifteen months and loved the experience. To some extent though, when you are reliant upon buses and trains to get you from place A to place B, you do isolate yourself from much of what is going on around you. That wasn't to say that backpackers didn't make the effort to integrate with the locals, a lot did. The difference was that on a bike, I integrated for every minute of my whole journey and for me that was the most enjoyable part of it all.

I had no desire to see any more markets or religious

icons, the most valuable and satisfying thing for me was to experience the day-to-day life of the people I met along my journey. There was a huge curiosity factor when I pulled up by a street cafe for a drink. It was quite normal to sit with the owners at their request and chat, usually in sign language. Cynthia was a major curiosity in her own right, she attracted a group wherever she was parked up. Upon entering a shop in Vietnam, I'd still hear her klaxon sound from outside and would be met by wide grins on my return. There were two instances where the locals really went beyond the call of duty to help me. On one occasion a young girl, who I had asked for directions, got on her scooter and escorted me to where I needed to turn off. The second time was in Sa Đéc, I had just arrived and asked a feller and his son about accommodation for the night. Without batting an eyelid, they got on their scooter and rode in front taking me to a superb hotel where the staff were unbelievably kind.

Being thin and linear in shape, Vietnam didn't have much space but it was still large enough to accommodate ninety million people. Given the topography, including the mountain region further north, there was only so much room for people to live and consequently, they congregated along the roads and water courses. Vietnam had a population that was some six times the size of Cambodia. Cycling through the Delta, I noticed that pretty well every village or town was linked to the next to form a continuous urban scape along every road. The villages were bustling, there was always something going on and it was clear that Vietnam was a wealthier country than Cambodia. There were a lot of building and construction projects in progress, notably bridges.

Commensurate with the size of population there were millions of scooters, what felt like an unbelievable number. After cycling for a few days, I was fully appraised of traffic methodology. For a start, it was absolutely fine to proceed against the traffic flow, and at all times traffic which entered the road from the left did so without sight or forethought, they just did it. In order to develop a successful cycling technique, 'weaving' was a priority. The key was to never stop, whether on a bike, scooter, vehicle or even as a pedestrian. If you kept going in a deliberate manner, all the traffic would weave in and around you. The first couple of times, it was quite nerve wracking, but I got used to it. Another rule of the road was that it was quite OK to go round a roundabout the wrong way. This was great since my survival rate increased by missing out junctions to get to the one I wanted. The noise was deafening, everyone seemed to have the horn on non-stop. I have to say though that the locals clearly recognised a foreigner when they saw one, very often they would 'shelter' me by letting me come alongside and protect me. They were also very respectful, well most were, so once I knew what was likely to happen, it wasn't too bad. Cycling into Saigon was not as bad as London, İstanbul or even Bangkok.

I stayed in Saigon only for a couple of days, but it provided a break from street food. Saigon was expensive and a typical big city, with a population of eight million (similar to Bangkok). I was advised to stay in Districts 1,3 and 5 which formed the modern downtown core, with all the fancy hotels and high-rise offices. It was worth being there just to see the traffic, strangely there were no tuk-tuks.

From Saigon to Hanoi the route was entirely Highway 1 and extended for roughly 1,800 - 1,900 kilometres depending on which road sign I selected. It was a long way regardless. Highway 1 in several areas was a poorly maintained road, it was barely the equivalent of an average A road in England. Cycling out of Saigon was very straightforward, and far simpler than Bangkok or İstanbul. As always, the locals rode by on scooters and looked on with mild astonishment or, as was more usual, made some crack or gesture and said hello. It was no surprise when a scooter pulled up alongside and the feller started a conversation in English. He insisted on buying me a Pepsi and during the interlude he told me that his name was Parat, he was eighty-two (although looked sixty) and used to work for an American Company as an interpreter. He took me to meet his family, we had iced coffee and then he took me for a quick trip through his village before saying goodbye as I re-joined Highway 1. Patience, politeness and respect were key words in Vietnam.

It took two days to reach Phan Thiết, which was a coastal port city. By chance I came across a KFC, an ideal place to regain a few calories. Having parked Cynthia, I walked in to a cacophony of noise and activity. I had gate crashed a children's birthday party which was in full flow over the two floors. Waiting for my order, some of the kids noticed this rather strange individual sipping a chocolate thick shake. As kids do, their natural inquisitive streak came into play and in their own way, they started to communicate and ventured ever nearer my table. I smiled at the parents as this unfolded and before I had my teeth clamped around the first chicken leg, several of them had moved onto my table. They were great and were having a ball watching me eat, one or two even spoke a few words of English. I was somewhat sad to let the moment pass, but it was time to move on.

I found a decent place to stay for the night before venturing out for something to eat. Parat had told me to visit Mũi Né which was a beach resort about twenty kilometres from Phan Thiet. The following morning, following a quick visit to the hospital as I had at last been bitten by a street dog, I followed the signs for Mũi Né. The Doctor insisted that I had a tetanus injection and the first of five rabies jabs. He asked me my intended route and gave me a list of every hospital to call into to get the remaining jabs. He even provided a letter of introduction for me to show each hospital when I arrived.

The road to Mũi Né provided easy cycling. Having crested a hill, I freewheeled down and in front of me was an expanse of ocean; The South China Sea. I immediately parked Cynthia against a coconut tree facing the ocean and slapped the saddle in delight. I felt a wave of elation take over. I suppose it was the realisation that I had largely cycled from the Atlantic to the Pacific. When I started my journey, I hadn't dared to look as far as Vietnam. It seemed an endless destination, but here I was watching the surf crash onto the golden sand. It didn't take much for me to hit the surf and go for a swim. The water was like a hot bath and I just felt so good. It was one of those moments that would have been great to share with someone, I felt a real sense of achievement and just let the waves wash over me.

There were loads of resorts and hotels extending along the bay. This was a quality resort location of an international standard. The beach was sandy and just about everyone was kite surfing. As I cycled along the main street, I was overwhelmed by the number of hotels and resorts, all of which had vacancies. I selected the Green Coconut Resort. It wasn't expensive, so I hired a bamboo chalet with a veranda and an ocean view. Palm trees were everywhere, the resort had a swimming pool, restaurant, bar and private beach. Believe me it was paradise. The weather was perfect, mid 80's with a warm easterly wind and no humidity. I spoke to an Aussie guy who owned one of the kite schools and he told me that the place was gradually getting recognised and that tourism was improving but that there was definite mileage in tapping the European market. Apparently, the majority of tourists were Russian. From experience, Russians rarely spoke to anyone. The French then formed the second largest tourist community, and like the Russians, they preferred to keep their own council. So, for myself and anyone else who wasn't Russian or French, the hope was to bump into some other Brits or Aussies who could usually guarantee a few laughs. Thankfully, there were a few of them around.

I met two French cyclists whilst heading towards Mũi Né. They told me that they were spending eight months cycling around Southeast Asia. After arriving in Hanoi, they had bought two bikes and set off from there. They had taken a bus for the midsection of the route as they had a timescale to arrive in the south. The following day I met two more cyclists, again heading south; it was like rush hour! Laura and Brant were from the USA and from their home in California (Big Sur), which is a terrific location, they had cycled across states to New York. It was a journey they completed in six weeks and was what most Americans considered to be a rite of passage. They kindly gave me a heads up on an alternative route into Nha Trang (my next destination). Brant was a very keen cyclist and both he and Laura had custom made bikes. He was well versed with Thorn and took pictures of Cynthia. We both had Schwalbe Marathon XR's tyres (which are no longer made, probably because they are so good). Brant had bought his set second hand with hardly any wear. In my opinion Schwalbe need to get on with manufacturing these tyres again as the replacements aren't a touch on the XR's! It was always good to meet cyclists on the road, to swap stories and discuss each other's bikes. These four were the first cyclists I had met since Turkey, although the Southeast Asian market was growing in popularity as a cycling destination. The two French fellers had bought their bikes for US$250 each and both said they were great for what they wanted.

Since arriving in Vietnam, I had been struggling somewhat with my energy levels. I put much of it down to the humidity, but by Mũi Né I was literally running on empty. I had nothing left in the tank at all and felt exhausted; I had travel fatigue. Well, whatever it was, I had decided after a couple days rest in Saigon, to take at least a week off by the beach after I arrived at the coast. My enforced stay was also influenced by the dog bite I'd received. Three of the five injections I could get while in Mũi Né and the other two I could get on the way north. For my second jab, I was invited into the surgery. Along the wall were nine chairs occupied by Vietnamese women and children. I started chatting to them and it was great, I had a ready audience to see the needle go in. Fortunately, the Doctor stuck it in my arm and nowhere more personal. Well, the combination of surf, sun and cold beer seemed to do the trick and I was on the way to recovery.

Midway through the week I received a text from my sister. As a consequence of the brutal rainfall that had fallen on the South West, it appeared that my house had not escaped and was flooded. Once I had telephoned my insurers to grant my sister effective power of attorney over the claim, she did a superb job continuing to coordinate what had been going on for my benefit. I was also indebted to my mates John, for his advice, and Quent particularly, who literally dropped everything to visit my place and prepare a claim report on the same day. You could not buy these kinds of mates and I knew I was very lucky to have them. So, while the claim was being collated, and the damage was assessed, I decided to stay in Mũi Né for another week. It ensured that I was readily contactable, since on the road it was not always easy to find an internet café. It also allowed me to get my 4th jab in as well. It had been my intention to spend two weeks in Ha Long Bay, but my situation reversed that. I still hoped to visit, however it would likely have to be for a shorter period. The manageress, who was a delight, booked me in for an extra few days, which was great as we had gotten to know each other quite well during my stay!

A week later and somewhat reluctantly, I cycled northwards out of Mũi Né to Nha Trang. I followed Brant and Laura's advice with the route they suggested kicking in about 30km from the city. It was effectively a dual carriageway. It was brand new with hardly any traffic, but it had the most superb sea views and was great to cycle. It was a gem of a route. It did take me a couple of days however, to crawl the couple of inches up the map to Nha Trang. I had hoped to arrive earlier, not that it mattered that much, but I had to negotiate a strong headwind all the way which reduced my progress considerably. At its worst I was struggling to make 6km per hour for a lot of legwork. Other than the headwind, it was a really good stretch of road. As I left Mũi Né, the land became almost semi-arid with dunes extending some way inland and cacti growing. Bougainvillea grew like a weed along the roadside and there was a shrub or tree which gave off a scent that reminded me of Provence. Gradually the land became more fertile and the scene changed to paddy fields with palm groves in the distance and mountains beyond. It was quite beautiful. Along the route there were glimpses of the coast and of course numerous villages and towns along 1A; the main route to Hanoi.

Life along the road continued to be interesting and fun. Truck drivers, shop keepers, road workers and men sitting around in the numerous cafes continued to chat, shout and wave. When pulling into a cafe, they would all gather round while I explained what I would like to drink. The women were lovely, always smiling, chatting and were very tactile. I had found this in Mũi Né. While all the testosterone fuelled twenty somethings were demonstrating their physical aplomb either by exercising on the beach or kite surfing, I just chatted away with very positive results!

There were loads of cafes although I was not sure how any of them made a profit. I generally liked to get an hour or two under my belt before a pit stop, and the day I left Mũi Né I did just that. I pulled into a cafe where six fellers were consuming Tiger lager at an alarming rate, well at

8am it appeared that way. They insisted I sit with them and would not hear of me leaving until I had drunk three cans of lager, so I did. They were also ripping a crab apart so again insisted I help them demolish that as well. This episode summed up long distance cycling; you never knew what would happen next. It was a given here that quite a few scooter riders would come alongside and slap me on the back by way of encouragement. It could be a bit dicey if I wasn't expecting it. The kids loved high 5's while I was in motion and held their arms out. Lads also liked to race me and overtake before heading off a side street, where they'd look back and laugh as they headed away. And yes, I did let them win.

On one occasion I stopped next to a collection and distribution plant where dragon fruit was the product in question. Dragon fruit is a mainly pink coloured circular fruit with pink 'fingers' coming off; hence the name, I guess. The inside contains a white coloured fruit with black seeds, it's very good to eat. The owner's daughter was called Anne and could speak perfect English. After meeting her mother and co-workers, Anne gave me four of these fruits to take with me which weighed in at about two kilos. This just demonstrated how generous the Vietnamese could be.

Hotels were plentiful and cheap. Rarely away from cities did I pay more than US$10 for a room, which was usually a double with a shower and air conditioning. On my second night out of Mũi Né I stayed in a room cantilevered over the ocean on both sides. At night I could listen to the swell and watch the fishing boats, it was wonderful. I frequently ate street food, although a big issue was the size of the chairs on the pavement. They were too small for me and this provided considerable mirth for the locals, especially when I misjudged 'landing' and the egg butty went flying! For breakfast, I could buy a warm baguette, two fried eggs, sausage meat, veg and spicy sauce for about 30p and it was very good. They also made coffee with condensed milk which I loved, not that I needed much incentive to spoon out and demolish a tin of that sugary stuff! In the evening it was potluck, but I generally selected something with noodles or rice, with water buffalo as the meat, or seafood. The girls often brought me crayfish or something else off the menu with a sauce and sat down to show me how to extract the meat. Of course, it was quite usual to spend the odd night, or part of it, on the loo so the following day I could feel a bit under the weather and not really look forward to getting on the bike. On days like that I thought about people who were a lot worse off than me. I bet they would have swapped their situation for mine in an instant. With that thinking I got myself into gear, gave myself a verbal kick up the backside and started pedalling. Of course, after spending so much time in the saddle, the old tackle got a bit sore. I tried a variation of clothing and other tactics to provide a bit of relief, but all was to little avail. I found the best solution was to flip occasionally from one side of the saddle to the other side. It seemed to work.

I saw from the date on my watch that Christmas was rapidly approaching, not that it felt like it. I was surprised that shops were selling Christmas trees and tinsel. So, to get into the festive spirit I bought some tinsel and decorated Cynthia. I was not sure where I'd be on the day, because of the headwind I couldn't see me making it to Ha Long Bay or even close. It didn't matter because the weather up there wasn't that great, Hanoi was only around 18°C which was positively freezing by Vietnamese standards!

The cycle north of Nha Trang to Qui Nhơn was excellent. Coastal views abounded and as with much of the topography along AH1 (the main route) the landscape was gently undulating. Qui Nhơn itself was a medium sized city with a long beach which gently sloped downwards. It bore some similarities to Nha Trang, despite being behind in terms of development and marketing. It certainly had potential. I stayed at Au Oc 2; Au Oc 1 was just up the road and fronted onto the main coast road opposite the beach. Either place was ideal for backpackers. Sandwiched in between was the Kiwi Experience (a hostel and café), which offered dorm accommodation for US$4 a night! If I was in need of a little western style food, this was the place to go! The Kiwi Experience, or Barbara's as it was also called, was a focal point for foreign travellers so it was a great place to get some first-hand information about surrounding routes.

The beach was great, but I didn't want to hang around too long after sunset. This was because the place was populated by rats, and big ones at that. Without a word of a lie, the creatures were about a foot long, as big as ferrets and some of the locals fed them so they were quite used to human company!

From Qui Nhơn it was about a 300km cycle to Hội An which lay some 30km south of Da Nang. Hội An was a must, despite being a quintessential tourist trap. It was a very attractive city that featured narrow streets with boutiques, cafes, and the lot really. There were also superb examples of French colonial architecture. The city was bisected by a river. Along the riverside were cafes where I could people-watch and enjoy life on the water. It was quite unique for Vietnam and was subsequently very expensive, but it was definitely worth a stop. Hội An lay a few kilometres from the beach, so for a couple of dollars, a lot of visitors hired cycles and explored the city. The Japanese bridge was a real highlight. I headed to the coast from Hội An and then followed the route into Da Nang. It was an excellent road, with sea glimpses, that avoided the city centre (and subsequent traffic) and allowed me to follow the beach right to the end before turning left and cycling around Da Nang Bay; it was a terrific run.

Da Nang, Vietnam's third city, had a population of around a million. Unlike Saigon or Hanoi, tourism was the dominant source of revenue. Just south of the city along the road I cycled, there were examples of just how developed and tourism focused the local economy was. There was a Greg Norman Golf Resort and major international resorts owned by the usual suspects like Hyatt etc with more in the pipeline. Once I negotiated the Bay, which was very attractive, I was faced with a choice, to either go through a tunnel or take the mountain pass. Well, the weather was good, I had the sun on my back, so I took the latter and was glad that I did. Although it was a three-mile climb (which I walked), the scenery was stunning. It was a place where the mountains literally met the sea. There was a leper colony set amongst the lower reaches, which was the last of its type in the country. This was told to me by a delightful Vietnamese lady on a scooter who passed me coming down the mountain. She managed to sell me a bit of jewellery for good measure too!

I stopped just short of Huế, which was some hundred kilometres from Da Nang. I arrived there the following morning which gave me a chance to look around and find somewhere to stay. Huế was a very popular city for travellers and a good stop off point. Most congregated around the old quarter, where there were shedloads of small hotels and hostels. It was also a good place for onward travel. I stayed in Huế for Christmas Day and Boxing Day. Christmas was a non-event in Vietnam although a number of hotels and businesses still got decked out in Christmas cheer purely for the tourists. I managed to call home and speak to my family, a second call to my son Nick really made my day. Chatting in a hotel lobby wasn't ideal, especially when the locals were massing in noisy discussion. They would get increasingly emphatic when trying to make their point and synonymously the decibel rate would rise dramatically.

I mainly hung around the backpackers' hostel where the food was pretty good, and the service was even better. It was in Huế that the weather turned, it started chucking it down every day. It appeared that the mountain range I traversed between Huế and Da Nang acted as a buffer of sorts. I had met a few cyclists on route, all were heading south. Without exception they had all taken either the train or bus from Hanoi to Huế. The reasoning varied from poorly maintained roads, bad weather and little to write home about in terms of scenery. Well, the weather was incentive enough in Huế for me to consider bussing it north but then I had set in my mind that I wanted to cycle as far as I could. The following morning was clear and warm, so I saddled Cynthia up and headed out making 130km (it must have been all that spaghetti I ate!). Hanoi was around 630km from Huế so I still had quite a way to go. It was from here things took a downturn. The weather closed in, and I met strong headwinds and lashing rain every day. It was relentless and reminded me of cycling through north Holland and Germany at the beginning of the trip. The cyclists' reports were also correct about the state of the roads. It was bad and very muddy. I couldn't comment on the views since I couldn't see anything! I eventually made it to Vinh, some 370km north of Huế, without a dry piece of clothing in the locker and feeling very cold.

With a lot of cursing and hard pedalling I eventually arrived on the outskirts of Hanoi, I was still soaking wet and cold. The previous evening two local fellers had undertaken a personal challenge to cut through and remove my Kryptonite bike lock, which had seized up after nine months use. In doing so they treated Cynthia with the utmost care, despite the somewhat agricultural approach to the task which was undertaken in a roadside shack that doubled up as their workshop.

I was anxious to avoid any morning traffic going into the city centre, and so made an early start. I checked Cynthia, she had no lasting damage. The guys who removed the lock were, like many of the tradesmen I met in Asia, very resourceful in limited conditions, working from sheds or on the roadside, they always got the job done; there was always a way. As I lifted a plastic poncho over my head, with the rain still pouring, I checked the panniers, made sure the passport was where it should be, and turned the handlebars once again towards the road. Constant rain and early starts had never been an issue, but the rapid drop in temperature since heading north of Huế had continued. I was used to cycling in tropical heat, even in December, and the sudden chill of winter caught me unawares. I just layered up as best

I could and cycled that bit more aggressively. I arrived in Hanoi on New Year's Eve and after finding a small hostel, I secured Cynthia near the reception. After tucking her away safely beneath the stairs, I found my room and headed for a hot shower.

Hanoi was a fascinating city and quite different from Saigon. It was quieter and more formal. The architecture was more heavily influenced by the French colonial style and had a lot of character. Whilst the main commercial heart of the country lay in Saigon, Hanoi was the administrative centre. The old quarter, which lay just to the north west of Hồ Hoàn Kiếm lake, was the place where I reacquainted myself with the Jomo cafe (having got to know their other branches in Vientiane and Luang Prabang). It was only a short walk from the hotel, and it felt wonderful to get good coffee and once again reintroduce my internal organs to a giant waffle soaked in fresh whipped cream and maple syrup. Could there be anything better?

My overriding priority was to buy some warm clothing. The locals were muffled up like it was -50, although, in the space of a few days the temperature did go down from roughly 30°C to 10°C which was a noticeable difference! I managed to buy a sweater that fit but I had no chance of buying jeans. I was 6ft 2in and anyone over 5ft 6in or who had a waist over 32 inches could forget it. In every shop I was met with a chorus of "No clothes your size"! So, I continued to walk the streets in shorts. Any branded jackets, even approaching my size, didn't look like the real deal. As I was only planning to remain in Hanoi for a couple more days, I decided not to bother and instead walked quicker to keep warm. My stay did allow me the chance to celebrate my 62nd birthday, which of course included a visit to the Jomo Café.

I reluctantly decided to return to England. My original plan had been to meet up with Nick, in Hong Kong and then head through China, Japan and onto Canada. Normally such change of plans would be made on the grounds of ill health, family issues or loss of interest, none of which applied in my case. I had heard from the letting agents that, following severe flooding, my cottage was taking in water that was likely to incur considerable expense which otherwise would have been used for travelling. I did not have a lot of faith in the agents and since there were no family members or friends to call on, I decided that Hanoi would be my last stop.

I contacted Nick who was now working for Cathay Pacific and he arranged a flight from Hanoi to Hong Kong. We were both disappointed at the outcome as we were looking forward to catching up. He managed to get me a first-class ticket which was real luxury. The airport staff in Hanoi were also very helpful with Cynthia. As was usual when packing Cynthia for a flight, I had to take the front wheel and pedals off and empty and repack the panniers. This involved throwing a lot of my gear away and condensing what was left into two, instead of four, panniers. While I was going through this process, the airline found a suitable cardboard box for Cynthia to go in and supplied me with copious amounts of clingfilm which I wrapped around her for the final time.

I flew out from Hanoi on the 4th January and was treated to three days hospitality at Hong Kong airport, since I only had a standby ticket back to London. Unfortunately, my arrival at the airport coincided with the busiest period after the Christmas holidays. Virtually all of the Asian student population (or so it seemed) converged on the airport, waiting to be decanted to London, Sydney and North America for the new academic term. There were four flights a day with Cathay Pacific to London, all were full, every day! I eventually managed to get a seat on the third day, after crashing out in the airport for two nights. Mine was not the only delay. In fact many on standby were in a worse situation, spending up to four days in the airport. I hooked up with a feller from Torquay who had 'lived' in the airport for a couple of weeks. He told me he had been deported from Singapore and was looking to clear his name before returning and continuing to earn a crust busking. The Hong Kong authorities would not give him permission to enter, so he stayed in the airport. Tim was quite a character, ingratiating himself with the airport staff by picking up litter and collecting trolleys throughout the day, all done with a smile, long dreads and barefoot!

A day trip around Ankor Wat

I only stopped for a chicken leg!

The school day begins - Vientiene, Laos

Cynthia's first sight of the South China Sea

Made it, the Atlantic to the Pacific (well South China Sea)

Cynthia decked out for Christmas, Vietnam

13

HOMECOMING

Well, what can I say about Cynthia! What a girl, my admiration for the quality of her build goes to the chaps at Thorn who built a masterpiece of a bicycle. The Nomad is a cracking machine, bombproof. Although I didn't quite hit the hardcore conditions I found in South America, she had more than enough to deal with. She was quite simply superb. It is true to say she had many admiring glances along the way. Many other cyclists recognised the bike and took photos. During the approximate 10,300km covered (my computer went on the blink due to a faulty connection I think, so I cannot be exact), with regard to repairs needed for Cynthia, I had ten punctures (eight before India), two broken spokes in Turkey, a slashed rear tyre in the Czech Republic and a replacement saddle in İstanbul. Throughout Vietnam, I only needed to change the chain in Hội An. Given the distance travelled it was virtually nothing at all. My thanks to Thorn for producing British bikes that sit with the best in the world.

After eventually managing to resolve the flooding problem with my cottage, I re-joined my old company. Unsurprisingly, they insisted that if I were taken back, I had to stay with them for a minimum of four years and not even think about heading off somewhere else. That was fair enough and anyway, I was not in a position to argue. It transpired that work was very slack in the South West so they asked if I would relocate and develop the East Anglian region. I agreed, moving virtually overnight to Norfolk.

As fate would have it, having learned to play Bridge, I joined the local club at Downham Market. There, on one fateful afternoon, I met my partner, Flora. We have now been together for seven very happy years and after completing my work contract (which incidentally extended to five years) we moved to Minehead where we both play golf and Bridge and are enjoying our retirement. Cynthia has now been sold to a twenty-one-year-old who was planning to cycle from England to New Zealand. So, for her the journey continues. Flora resists the urge to ask the question "Would you like to go for a bike ride?" and if I get the urge to go anywhere on a bike again, I am reliably informed that I will need a tandem!

One way or another, bicycles have played a major part throughout my life. But I shall never forget, and shall always be eternally grateful, to that Doctor who decided to have one more prod around in 1951.

StoryTerrace

Printed in Great Britain
by Amazon

66582611R00129